contemporary
leather

contemporary
leather

ART AND ACCESSORIES—
TOOLS AND TECHNIQUES

DONA Z. MEILACH

HENRY REGNERY COMPANY
CHICAGO

For Mel, Sue, and Al

All photos by Dona and Mel Meilach unless otherwise credited.

Preface

Contemporary Leather is an eye-, mind- and idea-expanding book. Accustomed as we are to leather in many aspects of our lives, we need to be jogged out of our cliché-oriented thinking about how it is used. Leather can be used by anyone interested in exploring its infinite potentials. All objects shown in this book are handmade by craftsmen. Illustrated examples demonstrate the continuing attempt of the creative person to find new avenues for old materials and to use familiar materials in unfamiliar ways.

This book is intended to stimulate the use of leather as an expressive, decorative, functional medium; to show you how to use both traditional and nontraditional approaches; and to encourage you to expand the use of leather along artistic and utilitarian avenues. It is meant to break the bounds of traditional leather usage and to lead you into exciting areas for this ancient material.

Use Chapter 2 to help you find many sources for leather. Chapter 3 is a general reference section for tools, their use, and application to specific and general projects. In subsequent chapters, refer back to Chapter 3 for the tools and techniques you need to complete a project. New demonstrations and tools are introduced where necessary as in sections on knitting, macramé, jewelry, and collage among others.

Where ample information on traditional techniques such as tooling, coloring, braiding, lacing, and sewing is available in other sources, it has been elected to show new approaches and techniques rather than go into explicit detail on well-known processes.

It is also hoped that the tools and demonstrations will dispel any mysterious aura about who can work with leather. Because manufactured items are so abundant, many people think they must, but cannot, compete with this merchandise. The idea is not to compete, but to develop something unique and individual. If it is not as slick and perfect as manufactured goods, it may be just that rough, handmade quality that gives an object its appeal. Yet good craftsmanship should prevail, especially when items will be given hard use and long wear.

If you never make a leather item, understanding the processes of leather and its many forms will give you a new appreciation of this material and its multiple uses.

Contemporary Leather is for artists and craftsmen who work in other media as well as for those who work in leather. Art and craft teachers for primary grades, high school, college, and golden age groups will find both artistic and practical items to satisfy almost every taste and ability. Hobbyists and full time leather craftsmen will discover a wealth of ideas.

Acknowledgments

Gathering material for this book has taken me from one coast of the United States to the other and into Mexico. Artists and craftsmen who are approaching leather in a new creative way were not abundant, but once located, all were delighted to share their ideas. I am grateful to their ability and for their generosity and cooperation.

Those I was not able to interview personally sent photos, shipped, or brought their work to me for photographing. Many included detailed letters or tape recorded messages of how their work developed—both philosophically and technically.

I offer my deepest gratitude to the following people who prepared demonstrations for my camera, read portions of the manuscript, and generously gave their time and effort: Fred Borcherdt, Tucson, Ariz.; Jack DeCarolis, Chicago, Ill.; Murry Kusmin of Murry Leather Handi-crafters, Hyannis, Mass.; John Snidecor and John Cederquist, Long Beach, Calif.; Ruben Steinberg, Chicago, Ill.; Bruce Vetter of Renaissance Leather, Champaign, Ill.; and Robert Zyer, Crestwood, Ill.

My thanks also to Eudorah Moore, Curator and Director of the Pasadena Art Museum, Pasadena, Calif., and to Sol Gurevitz of the Field Museum of Natural History, Chicago, Ill., for sharing with me examples from their collections and exhibits.

I appreciate the help of Mr. Robert Stern of Weil and Eisendrath Tanners, Chicago, who took me on a personally escorted tour through his tannery and helped me to understand processes I had only read about before. The manufacturers, tanners, chemical companies, leather findings suppliers and jobbers who shared their experience and knowledge are too numerous to list, but my thanks to all of them for their help and guidance.

Special thanks to Ben Lavitt, Astra Photo Service, Chicago, Ill., for his consultation on all photography. And to my husband, Mel, my gratitude for his patience and expertise with the camera, while I demonstrated many of the techniques and uses of tools.

I wish to acknowledge my daughter Susan's role as traveling companion, secretary, and model. Marilyn Regula has my deepest respect and thanks for decoding my scribbled, revised drafts into a perfectly typed manuscript.

DONA Z. MEILACH

Contents

HEAD. Nancy Grossman. 17 in. high. 1968.
Leather over hand carved wood head.

COLLECTION, THE WHITNEY MUSEUM, NEW YORK.
PHOTO, COURTESY, CORDIER & EKSTROM, NEW YORK

CHAPTER ONE

New Creativity with Leather

We tend to take leather for granted. We live with it all around us. Our shoes, handbags, wallets, book bindings, belts, jackets, gloves, suitcases, and scores of other items usually are made of some kind of leather. As a result, we think we know something about leather and how to use it. But the properties of leather are so myriad that even those who have worked with it for years readily admit that its potentials can be tapped in many more ways than most of them have time to explore.

Today, much of the creative exploration in leather is being conducted not so much by manufacturers of practical leather goods or those who have been steeped in traditional approaches to leather, as by individual artists and craftsmen who are using this ancient material in ways that it has never been used before.

For years, craftsmen have been tooling leather for wallets, saddles, and belts in the Western style so familiar to the United States. And because these craftsmen have seen leather mostly in terms of tooling, they are frankly astounded at the new statements being made and are anxious to "try something different" themselves. Those who are working in new forms are discovering that leather has extremely at-

tractive qualities for the design-conscious, experimental mind seeking additional media for expression.

Many craftsmen and artists have contributed examples of their work to this book. Some have been working with leather in more traditional ways for years and only recently have tried new approaches. Many artists are trained and experienced in other media, but have become fascinated with leather because of its flexibility and variety of textures, grains, colors, and qualities. Leather is not a predictable material. Because of its organic nature, each skin is different, and even areas within one skin may react differently to shaping, carving, and coloring. Perhaps one of the most intriguing things about some leather is that when it is wet it reacts differently than when dry—the things you can do with it are really miraculous.

Depending upon the tanning processes employed, leather can be made soft as butter, supple as velvet, or nearly as rigid and solid as wood. If hardened by heat and pressure, it will retain a given form almost indefinitely. The tensile strength of leather makes it resistant to friction and ordinary changes of temperature that often weaken fibrous materials. Yet it is porous, so that

DRUM. Hide serves as
the covering for this drum. Leather
thongs hold the hide taut over
the carved wood frame. A piece of wood
is used as a key to tighten the thongs.
PHOTOGRAPHED AT THE
FIELD MUSEUM OF NATURAL HISTORY, CHICAGO

clothing made of it can be worn in nearly all climates.

In addition to these remarkable physical properties, leather has even more to offer: it may be sewn like fabric, carved like linoleum, cut like paper, shaped like metal, laminated like wood, tied like rope, and knitted like yarn. It can be stretched, compressed, molded, tooled, inlaid, and made translucent or opaque. It can be colored with various paints and dyes to a richness unattainable in many other materials. It has been used for covering walls and tiling floors. And in addition to all of this, leather has sumptuous textures that are improved by polishing and treating with preservative agents. Visually, it is ornamental, often having a high degree of luster and sheen. Tactually, it is irresistible and can have a luxurious nap or a smooth, hard finish.

What about availability? Leather is mainly a by-product of the food we eat. Most hides do not come from animals killed for their fur alone, but are taken from cattle, sheep, goats, and horses used by the meat packing industry. Some four hundred tanneries across the United States produce millions of square feet of leather each year, providing a livelihood for thousands of American workers. In addition, the United States imports millions of skins annually.

Leather was among the first materials used by prehistoric man. Our primitive ancestors used animal skins as adornment for their bodies or as protection against the cold, the thorns along forest paths, and the weapons of their enemies. At first, hides were untanned, stiff, malodorous, and perishable. Then, some genius discovered that hides could be made soft and durable by

DOLL. North Africa. Body, head, arms, legs, and purse all made of leather.
COLLECTION: MRS. ELVIE TEN HOOR, CHICAGO

SHADOW PLAY FIGURE OF TA MU. Donkey skin and rawhide figures were used in the Chinese theater as shadow puppets in the 19th century. Actual puppets are about 15 inches high, intricately cut and brightly colored, yet their purpose was to cast huge shadows on backwalls.

COURTESY, FIELD MUSEUM OF NATURAL HISTORY, CHICAGO

treatment with salt, bark, and vegetable juices. This process eventually became known as vegetable tanning. In some cases, the treated hides were softened by methodically chewing them—a domestic duty of the womenfolk. The processes begun by the ancients are similar to the ones used today, only today, leather tanning has been updated by advances in modern chemistry and machinery.

Through the centuries, the diverse uses of leather have filled every functional and decorative need from tents for nomads to reliquaries of saints. Rough leather cups from neolithic inhabitants of Britain were found buried deep in the earth in Smithfield, London, in 1867. As early as 4000 B.C. bas reliefs in Egypt show leather-dressers at work. Fifteen hundred years later the Sumerians used leather for tires and harnesses. In Crete around 1500 B.C. water, grain, and other household goods were stored in leather containers. Stools upholstered with goat skin were found in the

LEATHER SHIELD from India. 18th Century. The leather is rock hard and curved and laminated over a thin metal shape. It is painted in greens and golds.

PHOTOGRAPHED AT THE FIELD MUSEUM OF NATURAL HISTORY, CHICAGO

tomb of Tutankhamen. The Babylonians and Assyrians used alum, gallnuts, oil, myrhh, and sumac to produce three varieties of leather.

In the Far East there is evidence that dates back to antiquity of armor made by stitching lacquered hides together. From aboriginal cultures, drums, fetish figures, clothing, and shields made from leather are still in existence. Artfully decorated leather thong sandals have been unearthed from early Egyptian tombs that date back some 5000 years. These sandals are believed to have been prized possessions of priests and nobles who were in the courts of the Phar-

aohs. The early Greeks used leather for wine vessels, armor, masks, money, and window panes. And in Roman history Caesar mentions leather sails that were hoisted on ships from Brittany. During the Middle Ages leather items were as popular as plastic items are in our time.

The American Indian, using crude curing methods employing smoke and elks' brains, produced leathers that had vast and versatile properties. The art of decorative leatherwork, including carving and braiding, was introduced in America by the Spanish in 1520 when Hernando Cortez came to this country with his horses.

CARVED LEATHER BOX. Spain. 16th century. Abstract human, animal, and tree shapes with scalloped borders and hinge.

PHOTOGRAPHED AT THE FIELD MUSEUM OF NATURAL HISTORY, CHICAGO

LEATHER TOOLING. Mexico. 1970. Intricately tooled panel depicts the Olympic Games.

Leather tooling and carving, which flourished in the Spanish culture from the ninth to eighteenth centuries, was probably introduced in Spain by the Arabs. Today, the fine, intricate Mexican leather tooling is still a traditional craft, stemming from past generations.

In America the white man adapted the Indian's knowledge of leather and refined the deer and buckskin tannates. Today, we still have styles worn by famous frontiersmen such as Daniel Boone, Davy Crockett, and Jim Bowie.

The first tanning business in the United States was established in Plymouth, Massachusetts, in 1623, only three years after the first Pilgrims had disembarked. Peter Minuit, governor of New Amsterdam, in-

vented the first machine used in tanning—
a horse-driven stone mill for grinding oak
bark, the primary vegetable tanning material.

Perhaps the major impetus to the rapid
developments that led to present leather
industrialization began in the early nineteenth century when the English chemist,
Sir Humphrey Davy, discovered that other
trees besides oak could supply tanning
chemicals. These were the hemlock, chestnut, and mimosa trees, which were all
plentiful in America. At the end of the
nineteenth century tanning with chrome
salts was introduced and represented the
first change in the chemistry of leather

MATCH HOLDER.
Joy Lobell. This piece
shows modern uses
of leather and techniques applied to a
box form in suede,
combined with
feathers, wood, and
unconventional
stitching.

HANGING. Fred Borcherdt. 30 in. long, 5 in.
wide. Eight-ounce cowhide hung with leather
bells; lacing and design at top corners and
bottom added.

tanning in 2000 years. Chrome shortened the weeks-long process of tanning leather to days and produced a greater overall uniformity in leather as well as a greater variety of performance characteristics. Consequently, there followed a manufacturing boom in shoes and other leather products.

The tanning industry flourished in forested areas where trees, needed for tanning agents, existed and near rivers and lakes on which hides easily could be transported. We all remember pictures from our history books of settlers paddling their hide-loaded canoes up the river to a trading post. Unfortunately, the rivers also were used to rid tanneries of waste materials. Today, new chemical agents are continuously being researched to help eliminate these wastes from our polluted waterways.

As our contemporary tanners constantly search for new ways to improve the quality of leather, designers, artists, and craftsmen continue to evolve new uses for it.

Whether your interest is sculpture, needlework, fashion designing, painting, knotting, weaving, sandalmaking, accessories, teaching, or simply searching for something new to tackle, you will discover an assortment of ideas in these pages. None of the projects is necessarily meant to be copied; rather the artist has shared his ideas and methods to help you begin. The purpose is to stimulate, not to emulate, creativity.

PORCUPINE CHUTE. Elisabet Siewert-Miller. 18 in. diameter. Leather and fur assemblage on wooden plaque. Assembled with glue and findings.

COURTESY, ARTIST

This assortment of leathers illustrates various shapes, colors, textures, grains, and fur applicable to projects described throughout the book. Leather offers unusual qualities, unmatched by any other medium, which are adaptable to expressive, decorative, and practical objects.

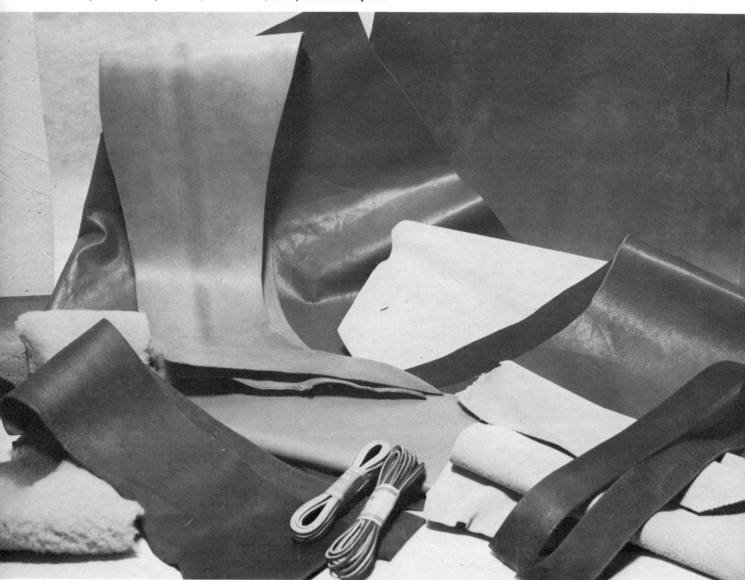

CHAPTER TWO

Learning about Leather

The first questions asked by the potential leatherworker are: where do I get leather? and what do I ask for?

Once bitten by the leatherworking bug, you'll find your first source of leather as close as your nearest closet. An old belt, worn-out shoe, outmoded handbag, scuffed suitcase, old suede jacket, broken equipment case, and worn gloves can all be dismantled and reused as scrap leather. To help you to recognize different types of leather, cut up these scraps from your closet and glue them to form a collage. Wet some belt leather and make imprints in it with the end of a tool such as a hammerhead or fork tine; that's what leather tooling is all about. You'll discover that shoe leather is thicker and handles differently than garment and belt leather. Glove leather is soft, supple, and smooth; other leathers may be hard, heavy grained, and coarsely textured. Some of the scrap will cut easily with a household scissors; some will require a heavy knife or a razor. All types of leather should hold together with household glues that specify leather bonding.

If you want new leather, consult the classified pages of your telephone directory. Look under (1) arts and crafts suppliers, (2) leather, (3) tanners, and (4) shoe findings and suppliers. If you live in a rural area, write for catalogs from mail order sources listed in the back of this book.

Arts and crafts suppliers frequently stock skins and some tools. Tandy's is the best-known in this field and has a wide variety of leather and tools. They have several stores throughout the country for both personal and mail-order shopping. In addition to skins many arts and crafts suppliers have precut straps for belts, pieces for purses, and leather in rectangular sheets. Many fabric shops and fabric centers of department stores carry leather for sewing vests, purses, skirts, and jackets. Precut leather fringe is also available by the yard in a variety of colors.

Under "leather" in the classified pages, you'll find several listings; the first one to investigate is marked "leather findings and suppliers." These dealers mainly supply the shoe industry. In addition to stocking shoe leathers, which are quite varied, many suppliers also buy odd lots of leather from tanneries and stack them up in a wild assortment of types, colors, and sizes for sale to anyone. A "findings" company also will sell quality tools, glues, tacks, stains, lacings, and finishing materials, which will be discussed later. The "findings" supplier's prices generally are a little lower than those of the craft supplier.

To begin, you probably have leather you
no longer use in your closet. Cut it apart,
wet it, dry it, shape it, glue it, texture it
to learn how many personalities leather has.

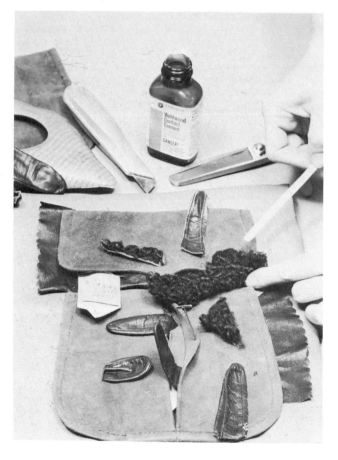

Next, check the "leather jobber" listing.
You might also look under "leather whole-
salers." These jobbers may carry only a
specific kind of hide such as garment
leather, as opposed to the kind of leather
used by manufacturers to make wallets,
purses, and shoes. A quick phone call to
the jobber will tell you if he has the kind
of leather you need; if not, he will probably refer you to a source that can help you.
Don't let the "wholesale" label frighten
you. Jobbers usually have two prices: one
for the bulk buyer and another for the person who needs only a few skins.

Another good leather source is a tannery, which may be listed under "tanners"
or as a subhead under "leather." The tannery, the place where hides are processed
and made into leather, frequently has scrap
and larger skins that are rejects from custom orders—all quite adequate for the art-
ist-craftsman's use. You can usually buy
leather at a comparatively low price if you
deal with a tannery. With the increased
use of leather by individuals, many tanneries have opened small retail outlets,
which may or may not be listed in the
classified listing of the telephone book.
Call the tannery to find out about their
current selling policies.

For a list of tanneries in the United
States and a variety of other information
and booklets, write to the Tanners Council
of America, 411 Fifth Avenue, New York,
New York 10016. Or refer to the Thomas
Registry in your local library for tanneries
throughout the United States and, specifically, those within easy distance of your
location.

The fourth listing, "shoe findings and
suppliers," may duplicate some of the
names under the "leather findings" listing.
However, many shoemaker suppliers simply don't think of being listed under
"leather," and in some cities there are so

Leather is similar to paper in that it can be cut and stretched by simply folding and cutting. A 2- to 3-ounce vegetable-tanned leather immersed in warm water and suspended over a glass to dry overnight will retain a three-dimensional sculptural shape.

few shoemaker suppliers that the classified book doesn't use that heading.

Once you begin your hunt for leather it is only a matter of research. Ask one dealer to recommend another for the kind of hides you might need; all are extremely helpful.

In your search you'll also discover leather suppliers listed in magazines that cater to teachers, craftsmen, and artists. Some of these are: *Arts and Activities, Handweaver & Craftsmen, Craft Horizons,* and *The Craftsman.* Write to any one of the leather suppliers advertised in these magazines and ask for their catalog and samples, which usually are free but may cost 25 or 50 cents.

For scrap leather cultivate your local shoe repair man, uniform maker, bookbinder, manufacturer of items such as wallets, suitcases, and purses. These leatherworkers have scrap that you can put to a wide number of uses. Your shoemaker, especially, can be a big help, sometimes putting your leather order in with his own, thus allowing you the price break of large-lot buying.

The same kind of cutting may be adapted to leather clothing design.
COURTESY, CRAFTMAKER, LTD.

HOW LEATHER IS SOLD

The first few times you buy leather it's natural to make the mistakes of buying what you really don't want or need and paying too much for it. These mistakes are part of everyone's learning process, so keep your first purchases small.

Leather is sold in whole or half skins, except side or shoulder pieces, which are sold by the piece. Leather is not cut to measure or patterns. Skins and sides are sold by the square foot. Because each hide is different and unevenly shaped, one wonders how it can be accurately measured. But the final step at the tannery is to put the hide through a measuring machine that drops finger-like projectiles around the skin and mechanically yields its square footage. The size is marked on the flesh side of the hide, and the total cost is calculated by multiplying the size by the price per square foot.

Size markings can be confusing. Markings are stated, for example, as 8^1, 8^2, 8^3, which means 8¼ feet, 8²⁄₄ or ½ feet, and 8¾ feet. Do not confuse 8^1 as 8¹⁄₁₀ feet. Decimals are not used in measuring leather.

The thickness of leather is stated in ounces, 1 ounce equaling ¹⁄₆₄ of an inch. Therefore, if you buy a 6-ounce cowhide,

the thickness will be approximately ³⁄₃₂ of an inch. Thicknesses vary from a 1-ounce piece at ¹⁄₆₄ of an inch to about a 10- to 13-ounce size that will measure about ³⁄₁₆ of an inch thick. Thicknesses that measure over ³⁄₁₆ of an inch may be sold by the pound rather than the square foot.

Some tanners also indicate weights of hides with the letters "L" for lightweight, "LM" for light medium, "H" for heavy. In addition "grade" marks, such as A, B, C, D, DX or 1, 2, 3, 4, may appear on a skin. Grades have no bearing on wearing quality, rather they indicate the condition of the grain of the hide in regards to coloration, natural markings, and surface scratches among other exterior signs. Skins carefully selected from one breed of animal are basically the same quality because of the selectivity and controlled tanning processes.

SHAPES OF HIDES

We have already mentioned that leather is sold in whole or half skins, side or shoulder cuts. As you buy and work with leather, you'll observe the various shapes of the hides. You'll also discover that some portions of the animal are better suited for working in certain techniques. For example, for forming and stretching leather,

Scraps of leather from policemen's uniforms and other sources are combined with suede and gears for this collage by Ruben Steinberg.

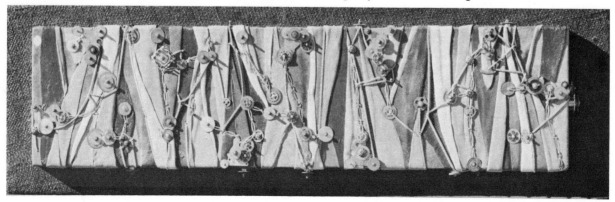

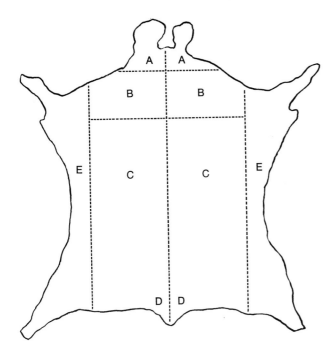

belly leather is more pliable than backs and sides. Backs are often used for strong strapping. Sides are used for clothing such as vests, jackets, and purses. The above gives you some idea of how a skin is subdivided and what these divisions are called. The entire piece is a full hide, usually referred to as the "skin"; half of it is a half hide. The entire skin is thickest at the center, thinning out toward the edges. Side cuts are marked (A) head, (B) shoulder, (C) back, (D) tail, and (E) belly.

SOLE AND GARMENT MEASURES

Another measure for leather is figured in "irons." One iron is equal to a piece measuring $\frac{1}{48}$ of an inch thick. The iron method of measuring is used for shoe sole leather. Sandalmakers will use the thickness of their choice, but most popular is a 9- to 10-iron leather, which is about equivalent to a 12- to 13-ounce cowhide and $\frac{3}{16}$ of an inch thick. Some sandalmakers use up to a 14-iron leather to give longer wear. You will learn more about this in Chapter 11 on sandalmaking.

For making fabric garments, patterns call for a specific number of square yards, which may be measured from a bolt. Figuring yardage for leather is a little tricky because of the limited sizes of the hides. However, there is a conversion formula for estimating yardage in leather. If a pattern suggests material with a 36-inch width, multiply the yardage needed by the number 9. Multiply your answer by 15 percent, which represents a cutting waste allowance. Then add your required yardage to this number. For example:

A poncho pattern calls for 4 yards of 36-inch-width fabric. So multiply: $4 \times 9 = 36$. Next, multiply this answer by 15 percent for the waste allowance: $36 \times .15 = 5.40$. Add 36 to 5.40 and the result is 41.40 square feet of leather required.

For patterns that call for a 54-inch width material, use the number 13 instead of 9 in the conversion formula, but don't change any of the other steps.

Obviously the skins must be in sizes that will adapt to each part of the pattern. So, if possible, place your pattern on the skins before purchasing them.

FROM HIDE TO LEATHER

As you begin to buy leather you will come across many words and phrases that you will want to add to your vocabulary and knowledge. You'll hear terms such as oak-tanned, vegetable-tanned, and chrome-tanned hides; splits and grains; cowhide and suede; flesh side, full, and top. All of these are confusing at first, but they are easier to learn if you know something about the procedure for changing raw animal hide into leather—the tanning process.

First, you must always remember that genuine leather originates from animal hides. When the hide or skin is removed from the animal, the water content along with bacteria and enzymes begin to deteriorate the material. If left to dry out, the hide becomes hard and brittle and of no commercial value. However, if the hide is treated with various tanning chemicals and techniques, it resists the action of water and bacteria and does not decompose. The process of preserving the hide and restoring oils to it results in the material we call leather.

Preservation of a hide, therefore, must begin almost as soon as it is removed from the animal, usually in the packing house. Here the hides are cured by a salt or brine process, which protects them until they reach the tannery.

At the tannery the hides are washed and soaked to remove the salts and any foreign substances and to restore the fibers to a natural shape and condition preparatory to absorbing the tanning agents. Additional steps include loosening and removing the hair, defleshing the hide, and other machine processing, which results in a smooth-surfaced hide with a distinctive grain pattern.

Fascinating machines clean the hides, smooth the surfaces, and, finally, split each hide into layers. It is this splitting that produces top grain and split leathers. When you see "splits" advertised, you'll realize that these are one of the layers from under the top grain. It is easy to understand this splitting process if you take a piece of colored ¼-inch cardboard and split it into four or five layers. Only the top layer will be colored—comparable to top grain leather—and each of the other layers will be the same as splits of leather.

There is also a difference between top grain and full grain leather, which also originates during the tanning process. Top grain is the top layer of the smoothed skin, which is sometimes buffed and treated. Full grain refers to the cut layer in which the original grain has not been buffed, reduced,

or smoothed in any way. Definitions vary with tanners and manufacturers, so it is best to examine the material before buying it to be sure you get what you want. Splits may be pigmented with a solid coating to look like top grain.

After the skins are cleaned and smoothed they are tanned—the chemical process by which the hides are made soft and durable, strong and pliable. This involves reimpregnating the fibers with new chemicals to replace those lost through cleaning.

Chrome Tanning

The chrome-tanning process uses chrome salt solutions, which turn the skins a light blue-green. Almost all skins are chrome tanned today because this tanning process can be accomplished in a few hours and produces a leather that has properties suitable for a multitude of commercial products. Chrome tanning results in a leather that has great flexibility, long-wearing abilities, and a high degree of resistance to scratching, scuffing, and scarring. Consequently, it is the process used on hides that will be made into shoe uppers and garments. However, chrome-tanned leather also may be put through a vegetable-tanning process to give it the additional qualities of that process.

Vegetable Tanning

Vegetable tanning uses tree bark and extracts plus chemicals. Originally, tannin, or tannic acid from trees, was the sole agent for a vegetable-tanning process that required weeks. Today vegetable extracts are combined with chemicals to speed the tanning period and to produce rich, lightweight, very flexible leathers. Most shoe soles, luggage, upholstery leathers, and industrial belts are made from vegetable-tanned cattle hides. This process results in a firm, durable, and water-resistant product. You will often see leather sold as either

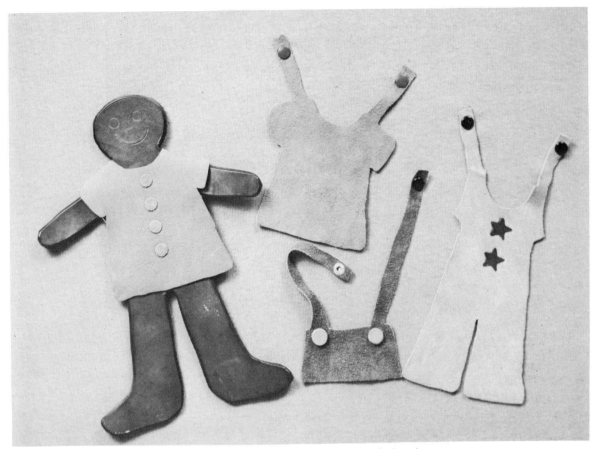

Sole leather is transformed into a leather doll and colorful suede clothes by Linda Vetter. The clothes can be snapped on and off for quick changes.

"oak tanned" or "vegetable tanned." For all practical purposes, the terms are synonymous because oak bark is one of the many vegetable-tanning agents.

OTHER TANNERY PROCESSES

In the tannery various processes give the hide a variety of leather finishes such as smooth, grained, suede, patent, and lustre. Suede is made by buffing the flesh side of the leather to raise a soft nap. To make a finer suede, the entire grain on the smooth side is buffed off. Both sole leather and soft-as-butter glove leather can come from the same animal; the tanning techniques are what render each hide different.

Coloring leather is also done in the tannery, although the craftsman can buy natural leather and do the coloring himself by the various methods described in Chapter 3. Both tannery-dyed leather and hides you dye yourself will not necessarily be uniformly colored. Leather, being a natural material, has certain fiber variations that cannot be changed by any method. These fiber differences often determine the dye penetration, but it is the variations in tone that give leather a unique quality.

After coloring, the last "wet" process in leather tanning is called "fat liquoring." This process restores oils lost during wetting. Then, the leather finally is dried by

ASSORTED ROUND CONTAINERS.
Joy Lobell. Details of fur,
feathers, and colored leather
over straight and pleated bodies.
Boxes are also lined with leather.
PHOTOGRAPHED AT DESIGN WEST, LOS ANGELES

any of several methods depending upon the tannery and the purpose to which the leather will be put. The leather pieces are stretched on frames that resemble curtain stretchers and then are placed in warm-air circulating rooms to dry. Additional finishing includes conditioning, buffing, coating, and several other specialized processes.

A visit to a tannery will give you a good understanding of leather production. However, because of high insurance costs, tanneries are reluctant to conduct tours. In addition, tanneries are not the most aromatic places to visit. But if you are genuinely interested, call a tannery office and a tour may be arranged for you; and don't forget to take your waterproof boots.

Barring the tour, it is interesting to mosey around the yard of a tannery, noting activity as the skins arrive and are baled in the chrome-tanned blue-green stage, waiting for additional tanning, and as they are packed for shipping.

Tanneries operate differently, of course. Some buy hides and process them in different ways for many purposes; others tan for a few special customers, always working with approximately the same formulas. Knowing which tanneries produce a certain type of leather can certainly minimize your searching time. If one tannery, for example, produces only glove leather, it is pointless to rummage through the leftovers for sandal or purse leather.

A NOTE ABOUT FUR

Several projects throughout this book were made with fur pelts in combination with leather. Fur is processed differently than leather. Although it is the animal skin without the hair removed, it must also undergo tanning processes to prevent deterioration. Fur processing will not be discussed here in detail. Suffice it to say that you can find many fur remnants and scraps from old clothing, coats, and hats in secondhand and rummage shops. New pelts are available where fabrics are sold or from furriers and furrier suppliers. Artistically and practically, fur is a naturally attractive and imaginative material to combine with leather. It may be glued and sewn, cut and pinned, and joined in the same ways as leather.

NAMING LEATHERS

About the only other terms you'll find confusing when you start to learn about leather, other than those already discussed, will be references to particular kinds of skins: cowhide, deerskin, sheepskin, latigo, horse's belly, and morocco leather among others. If it's any consolation, the average craftsman usually cannot identify the kind of animal a given piece of leather came from with the exception of cowhide. If he does call a piece by a specific animal name, chances are he knows what it is because that is what he ordered from the catalog or tannery. Craftsmen also know what use they want to put the leather to, and experience tells them the kind of leather that works best. Even those people who have sold leather for years are not always sure of the origin of a split, a piece of suede, or a shoe upper unless it has a definite grain such as alligator, snake, or goatskin. So don't let confusion about hide origin frustrate you. It is more important to find the leather that will do the job you want it to, and consulting the leather dealer is your best guide. Experience is your best teacher.

DETERMINING TANNING DIFFERENCES

Often, the craftsmen will want to know whether a given piece of leather has been chrome or vegetable tanned. This is particularly important when working with leathers that are to be stretched, formed, and tooled because only vegetable-tanned leathers are suitable for molding and shaping.

Cut a scrap from each of the leathers in question. A chrome-tanned piece of leather often has a beige or gray streak in the center layer where the coloring did not penetrate. A vegetable-tanned piece will be more uniform in color throughout the layers.

Another test is to dip both pieces of leather in warm water and fold them. The chrome-tanned piece will spring right back to its original state; the vegetable-tanned piece will hold the fold almost as a piece of paper would. In addition, wet vegetable-tanned leather has a distinctive slippery feeling unlike chrome-tanned leather. Try this test on two known pieces of leather, and you'll have little trouble determining the differences as you become more experienced.

STORING LEATHER

Leather should be stored in a clean dry place at moderate temperature. Warmth and dampness can cause mildew. Excessive heat, such as an area near a furnace, can cause the oils to dry out. Leather should be stored flat if possible. Otherwise, roll the skins over a large cardboard tube or hang them over a rounded shape. The idea is to avoid creases that may leave permanent sharp lines in the leather.

Small pieces of heavy leather can be stored flat in boxes, but make sure that there are no foreign particles between layers that might dent the surfaces of the skins. Prolonged exposure to sun may cause leather to fade and dry out, so try to keep finished pieces away from direct sunlight. When wrapping skins, roll them in heavy brown wrapping paper (to avoid dust and soil) with the grain side out so they don't wrinkle.

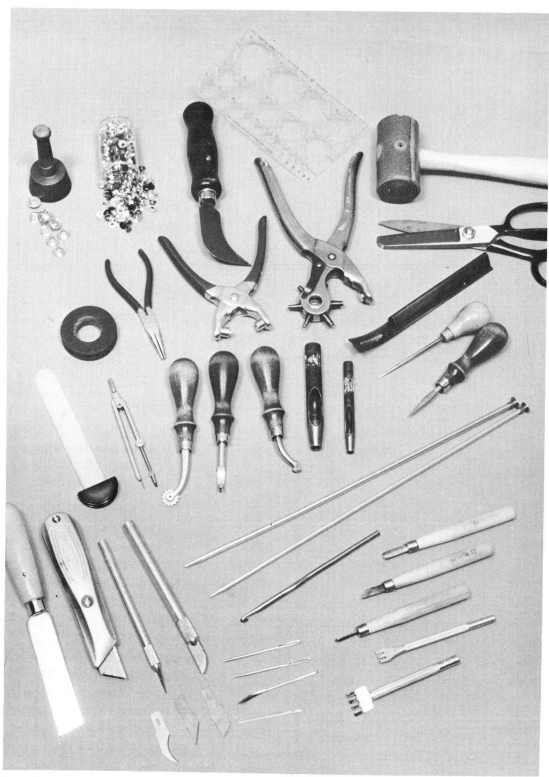

A variety of tools in this and subsequent chapters is associated
with leatherwork, but many are not. Shown are cutting instruments
used in many hobbies: knitting needles and crochet hooks,
ordinary scissors and leather shears, and items especially
applicable to leatherwork.

CHAPTER THREE

Tools and Their Uses

Because of the versatility of leather and the many ways it can be worked, assorted tools have been developed for specific purposes. However, don't let the array of available tools perplex you. Only a few may be used for any given procedure. For many processes you can improvise tools from kitchen utensils and your home workbench. For others, minimal special tools, readily available, make the job easier. Actually, tools recommended specifically for leatherwork are simple, unsophisticated, and inexpensive. If you really want to plunge in, you can readily be "in business" with a $50.00 tool budget. About a $5.00 tool expenditure can give you a good start.

In this chapter, tools used for various processes illustrated throughout the book are introduced. Examples of a finished piece, on which the tools and procedures were applied, follow each demonstration. Where additional tools are required for techniques discussed in subsequent chapters, these also are shown and demonstrated.

Specific tools for specific leather-working purposes are usually a must for the purist leatherworker. But the nonpurist feels free to use any tool for any procedure so long as it does the job. Wood and linoleum carving tools often are as effective as

traditional leather tools for some techniques. Dental and medical instruments accomplish some procedures beautifully. Artists' oil and acrylic paints may be applied to leather as easily as to canvas. You don't have to adhere exclusively to leather dyes to color leather. Cutting dies made from pipes and other formed metal have been devised by innovative craftsmen who want specific shapes without the cost of custom-made cutters.

Where can you buy leatherworking tools? The most complete selections are available from craft suppliers, shoe findings companies who cater to shoemakers and saddlers, and direct from manufacturers (see Sources). However, there are some tools that are not exclusively used for leather, and these often are available from your local hardware dealer. Such tools include cutting shears, revolving punches, drive punches, hammers, glues, stitchers, grommets, and rivets and their setters. These are the same as, or similar to, tools used by the person who works with canvas and plastic or uses leather in an everyday work context. Leatherwork tools usually are made of chrome, stainless steel, or highly polished tool steel that will not rust or stain wet leather.

A solid workbench and an organized method of hanging and sorting tools will facilitate your work. Good light and separate storage for glues, dyes, paints, and finishing waxes are also helpful. Tools should be kept dry to prevent rusting.

Tools are introduced here in order of probable use, beginning with those for cutting and punching leather. However, needs will vary depending on what you are making, so use the entire chapter as a reference to tools and techniques for all projects throughout the book. If you find tools that work well for you but are not shown here, use them.

Basically, the sequence for leatherworking is (1) designing, (2) cutting out and assembling, (3) coloring, and (4) finishing

with neat's-foot oil, saddle soap, or similar preservatives. You frequently may alter this procedure to suit the requirements of your particular project.

CUTTING AND STRIPPING

The primary requirement for cutting leather is a good sharp tool. A dull cutter is the greatest deterrent to a neat, successful job. The type of cutting tool you'll need depends on the thickness of the leather. Thin leather may be easily cut with a household scissors. A toothed leather shear is best for leathers up to about 8 ounces. Thicker leather generally requires a sharp-bladed knife, that is, a kitchen knife; an X-Acto or Stanley knife; or flat,

Cutting tools (*clockwise*): physician's scalpel, X-acto and Stanley brand cutters, which have a variety of interchangeable blades, wood carving knife, carpenter's wood chisel, electric saber saw with special toothless blade, household scissors, and leather shears. The shears has two blades; one has teeth that holds leather while the other blade cuts, yet no toothmarks remain on leather.

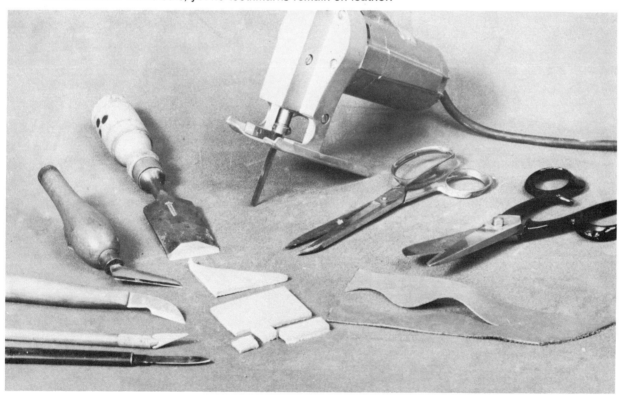

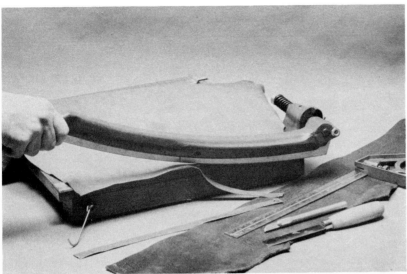

Thin leathers may be cut with a paper cutter. For almost any leather use a sharp knife, such as an X-acto or Stanley hook blade No. 1996A-5 or a square, round, or angle-pointed knife drawn along the leather using a metal straight edge as a guide.

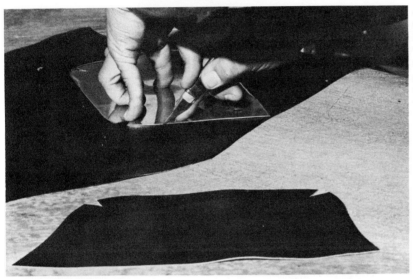

A metal template is the cutting guide for a bevel-pointed skiving knife. Templates are used whenever a shape will be cut several times. Cut templates from sheet metal using a tinsnip. Original patterns should be made from cardboard first.

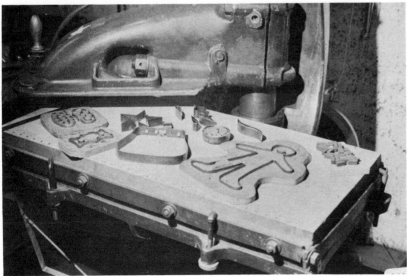

A clicking machine is used commercially for cutting shapes. Clicking time may be rented by a craftsman from a company that manufactures leather products. Straight line and shaped dies are made from sharpened metal strips mounted on a wood block. These cutting dies are placed over the leather, and the clicker head is forced down electrically over the dies so that the entire shape is cut out at once.

angled, or round-bladed leather-cutting knives. For cutting layers of laminated leather, you may use a toothed blade in a band saw or a nontoothed blade in a saber saw. Leather strips can be cut with any of these tools or with a draw gauge.

To prevent knife blades from dulling quickly, always back up the leather you are cutting with a piece of end-grain wood, Masonite, a square of rubber or asbestos tile, Plexiglas, or a piece of scrap leather.

Replace blades frequently to prevent burrs and rough edges. For resharpening nonreplaceable blades quickly, rub the edge lightly on the striking surface of a box of safety matches. This sandpaper-like surface is a fine abrasive that will keep blades keen without disturbing their cutting edge.

When blade edges dull, sharpen by whetting them on a clean oilstone. Work the edges, usually the one inside is flat and the other beveled, at the same angle at which the blade was originally ground. Start by using a fine-grade whetstone and finish with an extra-fine grade, available from your tool supplier or hardware store. A grinding wheel also may be used for sharpening cutting blades. For stropping, use a strip of heavy scrap leather.

For straight edge cutting, a metal T-square or other metal edge guide is best. To cut multiple patterns, make a template (the pattern shape) of thin sheet metal and grind the edges smooth. Anyone planning production cutting should be familiar with the function of a clicking machine.

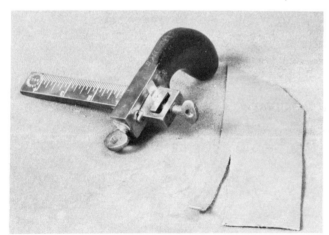

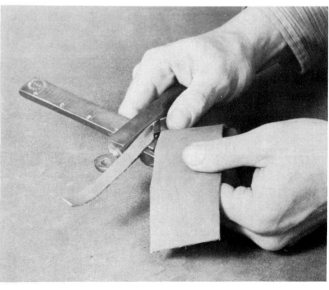

The draw gauge is designed to cut even strips of leather for straps, belts, laces, etc. It is a hollow-handled pistol grip tool with an adjustable slide bar along a ruler. A replaceable sharp blade, which tightens with a thumb screw, is in the bar. The blade can be slipped along the ruler to make strips from ¼ inch to 4 inches wide.

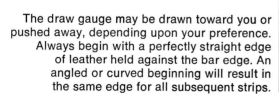

The draw gauge may be drawn toward you or pushed away, depending upon your preference. Always begin with a perfectly straight edge of leather held against the bar edge. An angled or curved beginning will result in the same edge for all subsequent strips.

Stripping narrow laces to wide straps may be done with the sharp knife against a metal edge using a piece of wood or other backing for cutting. If you cut on soft side-grain wood, cut across the grain, not with it. In many leather shops, belt strips are frequently cut with a 48-inch blade paper cutter.

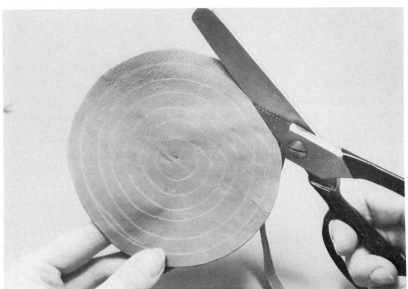

Long thongs may be cut from a circle (otherwise lengths of thongs are determined by the length of the hide), but it is difficult to get edges perfectly straight when cutting from a circle. Make several circles with a compass; then cut carefully, making a cross cut into every subsequent circle. To make the thong lie flat, wet and stretch it after cutting. Long thongs needed for macramé, knitting, lacing, etc. also may be made by skiving ends and gluing.

BIRD. Jack Kearney. Varied colors of scrap leather are cut, stripped, and overlaid on a wood and chicken wire armature to simulate the feathers of a bird. The head is made of carved wood.

SKIVING

Skiving means to shave down, or pare an edge. It is an important operation for many practical uses of leather. If you're making a belt, for example, the edges that go through the buckle should be shaved down so they slide through more easily. You would also skive the end of the belt that secures the buckle, so that it will be less bulky when it is wrapped around the buckle and adhered at the back.

Wherever you put two pieces of leather together, you could skive each piece, so that combined they are the same thickness as a single piece. Skive the edges to be joined for lacing, stitching, or riveting. This applies to pursemaking, putting straps in a sandal, the edges of a sculpture, and overlaps on a collage.

Normally skiving is done on the flesh side of a piece of leather about 3 ounces or thicker. When skiving on thinner leathers, there is a tendency to cut through. You can skive the ends of suede or glove-leather thongs before gluing them if you require lengths longer than any one skin for macramé, lacings, or knitting.

To skive, hold the piece of leather firmly against a hard, flat surface, such as a slab of marble, stone, or wood, which is raised from your work table. Working on a raised surface gives you room to angle the tool without scraping your knuckles. Hold the leather with your free hand behind the cutting blade, so if the blade slips, you won't skive your hand. Push the tool from you, cutting away the desired depth a marked distance from the edge. A steady pressure helps give an even bevel.

Skiving tools also may double as carving knives and are useful for making grooves when creasing and bending leather (described later in this chapter).

Tools for skiving, or shaving down, a leather edge are *(left to right)*: a head knife, also used for cutting heavy leather; a skife, often called a safety beveler; an X-acto side cutter blade; and a French skive.

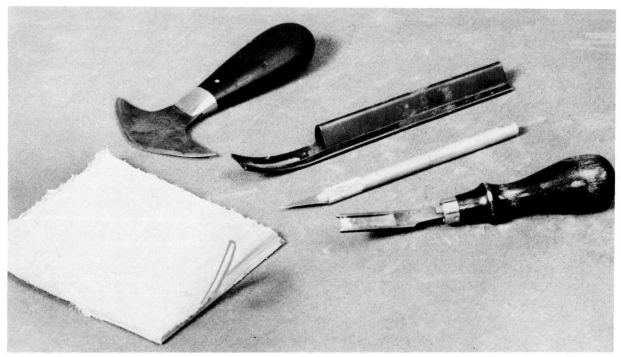

The skife has a curved cutting head, which is held at a slight angle to the leather and pulled toward you. Working on a cutting board allows you to angle the tool for the edge bevel desired. Replaceable blades are the same as those used in the Schick injector razor. Blades should be cautiously pushed out with an awl or other sharp pointed tool. Do not try to pull them out with your fingers.

Any sharp knife carefully held at the desired angle and worked with an even pressure may be used for skiving. Here an X-acto with an angled blade shaves the edge. The head knife *(at left, page 26)* also may be placed at an angle to the edge and pushed. An old-fashioned straight razor also works well. The sharp blade alone from a woodworking plane, hand held, works for belt ends if you hold the blade steady and pull the leather toward you.

The French skive operates on the same principle as a wood plane. Place the tool edge along the flesh side of the leather to be shaved and push to lift off excess material.

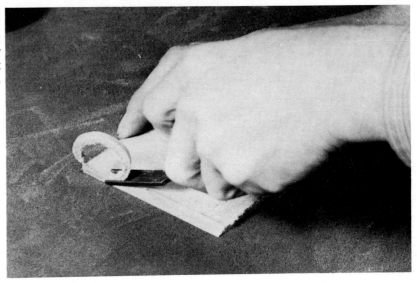

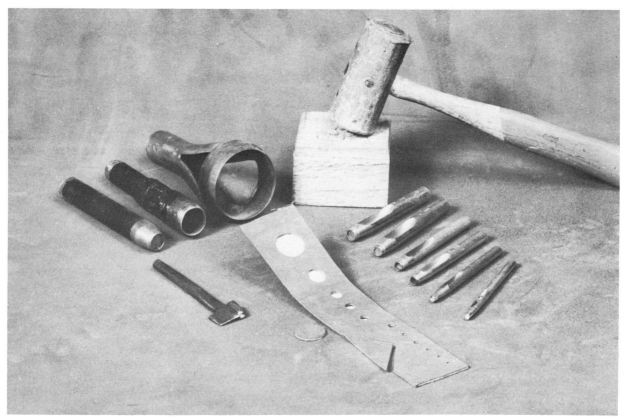

Homemade and manufactured drive punches are *(clockwise):* cutting chisel shaped to make buttonholes in a keyhole shape; water pipes ground, beveled, sharpened, polished, and case hardened; an arch punch; block of wood and rawhide mallet; round hole punches in graduated sizes. Leather strip shows holes made by punches.

PUNCHING

Punching leather with tools having pre-formed shapes is actually another phase of cutting. There are punches for circles, ovals, oblongs, C's, U's, and any shape you can fashion. Two types of punching tools are basic: (1) the revolving punch that works like a pair of pliers and (2) the drive punch that is driven through the leather with a mallet or spun through on the chuck of an electric drill.

Revolving Punch

The revolving punch makes holes the size of each of the six cutting tubes extending from it. It is limited to use at edges because of its short jaw length and is excellent for punching holes for lacing, eyelets, and rivets in thinner leathers. Revolving punches vary in quality and characteristics. Light weight styles have hollow handles, while heavier ones have solid handles. The finest type has a parallel structure jaw rather than a plier-type action. Some have tubes which are replaceable when they dull or wear out.

Drive Punches

Drive punches are placed on the leather (usually with the grain side up), which is set on a wood board or on a piece of scrap leather. The end of the drive punch is hit with a rawhide, wood, or rubber mallet. Never use steel hammers because they tend to splay the ends of the drivers. Sometimes two or three hits are required to drive the punch through a heavy piece of leather. Rubbing the cutting edge of the punch in beeswax or candlewax will make it much easier to drive through the leather. Sometimes punches go through wet leather more easily than through dry.

Drive punches range from a No. 00 that makes a 1/16-inch diameter cut to a No. 16 that makes a 9/16-inch diameter hole. Oblong punches range in length from 1/2 to 1 1/2 inches. Ovals are numbered in graduated sizes from the smallest at No. 1 to the largest at No. 16. Before punching, use a plastic circle template to determine the placement of the hole and the size required.

All punches are hollow and are wider at the top than the bottom. This permits the punched-out leather blank to slide up the tube and out the top. Should the punch clog, push the blanks from the bottom up with an awl or other sharp tool. In addition to ready-made punches, many craftsmen make their own odd shapes from pipes and forged steel, and the methods used are described in this chapter.

Tubes of the revolving punch snap around to yield six different size holes. Leather is placed, grain side up, between the tube and anvil of the jaws, and the handles are squeezed. On thick leathers, it is sometimes necessary to place a scrap of leather over the top of the tube and hit it with a mallet as with a drive punch. Unless the tube is held at a 90° angle to the leather, an angled rather than a straight cut may result. Always practice cutting on scraps. Larger holes have been cut with homemade punches *(left)*.

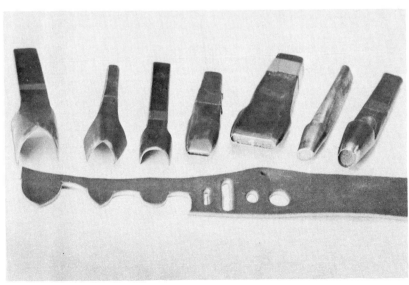

Other punch shapes include *(left to right)* a wide V shape, narrow V shape, and wide U shape, usually used for punching belt and strap ends. Different width shapes are available. Oblong and oval punches are used where straps, laces, etc. may be pulled through, but they also may be used for decorative purposes. Save the negatives from punchings for jewelry, collage, stringing, and decorating.

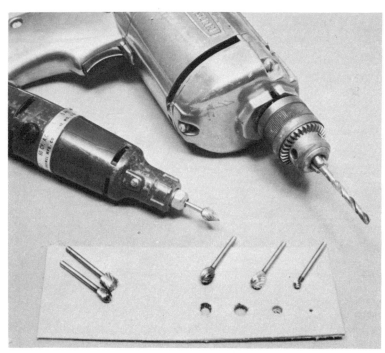

Electric hand drills may be employed for cutting holes in leather. A craft drill *(left)* has several different bits that will cut through leather. But because of the rapid rpm, you must be careful not to friction burn the leather. A portable electric drill may be used to drive round dies fitted with a mandrel that will insert into the chuck, *(right).* Bruce Vetter altered large, round-toothed wood dies by grinding off the teeth, beveling and sharpening the edges, polishing them with jeweler's rouge, and case hardening the tools. You may want to case harden some tools with Casnite, which is available from welding suppliers. With a removable mandrel attached to the die and fitted into the chuck, you can efficiently make multiples of holes in a hide *(see below).*

Kip, or half a hide, from which rounds have been cut with a punch, which was fitted to the chuck of a ½ inch electric portable drill. The hide was placed on a piece of plywood; then Mr. Vetter moved along cutting blanks to be used as peace symbol barrettes. The speed of the highly polished cutting edge simultaneously burnished the leather cut edge, so no additional finishing was required. These tools must be highly polished with jeweler's rouge to reduce friction that might burn leather. The leftover shape makes an interesting wall hanging.

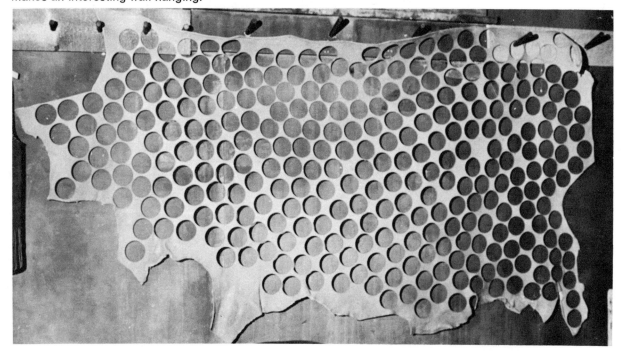

Homemade punches were used to make items below by Bruce Vetter. These punches are improvised from pipes, forged steel, and reshaped commercial dies. Group of round punches *(center)* have a mandrel stem that fits the chuck of a ½ inch portable electric drill. Mandrels and assorted size cutters are hardware store items.

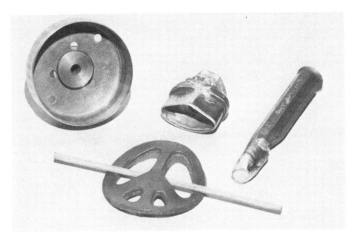

Series of shaped punches required for inner cuts of peace symbol. When driving these punches through the leather with a mallet, Mr. Vetter prefers to back up the leather with a piece of end-grain wood because it is less likely to damage the edge of the cutting tool than is side-grain wood.

Punches for making an oval barrette were improvised by Bruce Vetter. One punch *(left)* makes two oblong holes so that they will always be equidistant. Punch *(right)* cuts the outer shape.

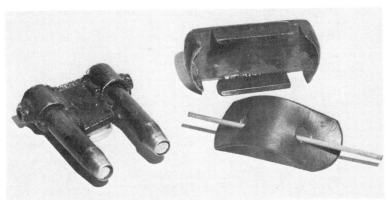

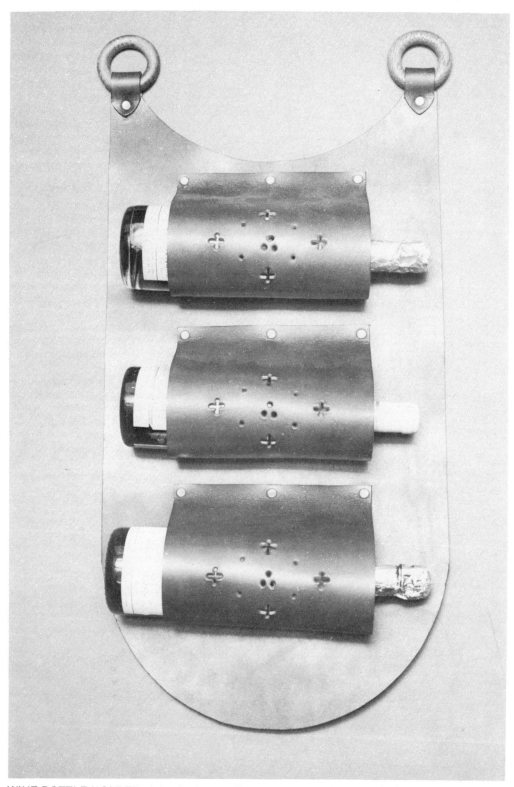

WINE BOTTLE HOLDER. John Anderson. Punches are used decoratively and functionally; the holes within each rack are made with oval or round punches. Holes also are required for the rivets that hold the suspended pouches to the backing and for the turnovers at the top that hold wooden rings. The leather used is morocco vegetable-tanned cowhide dyed brown.

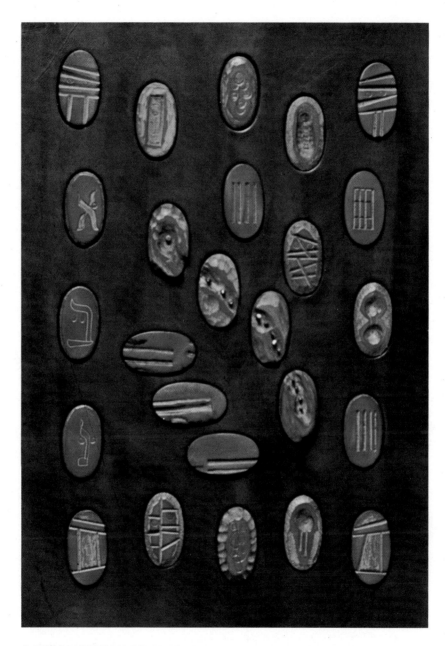

A RECOLLECTION OF JOURNEYS. Murry Kusmin. Oval shapes
punched from shoe leather are carved with woodcutting chisels and set
into a brown cowhide background with slightly larger punched oval holes.

ORNAMENTAL CHALICE. Murry Kusmin. Modern carving may be done with a narrow woodcutting tool. The artist has carved a simple light relief design in the plain surface of the leather.

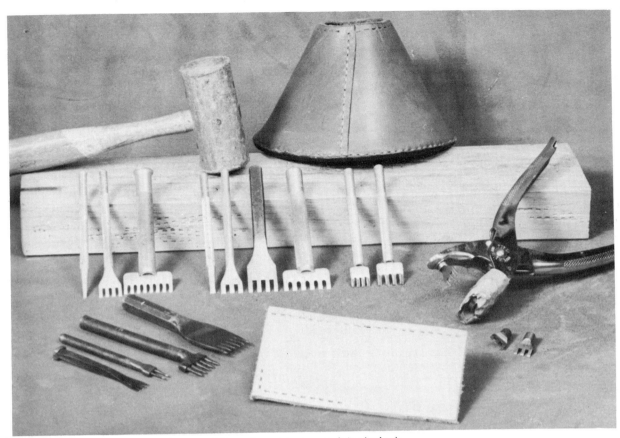

Assorted sizes, styles, and shapes of thonging chisels are *(clockwise):*
an improvised thonging tool made from a cold chisel; three sizes of round
prong chisels with 2, 5, and 6 prongs; standing *(rear)* straight prong
3/32 inch tool with 1, 4, and 8 prongs. One-fourth inch slits will be produced
by 1, 3, 4 and 6 prong chisels. Two at right have diagonal prongs. Pliers-
like tool has replaceable prongs. Anvil is covered with a piece of leather
to serve as a backing to make cutting easier. Leather showing evenly
spaced slits made by tool *(front)*. Rawhide mallet and oak two-by-four
for backing *(rear)*. Cone is joined with saddle stitch.

THONGING CHISELS

Thonging chisels (also called stitching
punches) are additional cutting tools. They
cut one or a series of small, evenly spaced
slits for lacing or stitching leather. Unlike
fabric, leather is almost impossible to penetrate with a hand needle, so it is necessary
to prepunch needle holes. In principle,
thonging chisels are similar to the drive
punch. The point of the chisel, like the
drive punch, is placed on the grain side of
the leather; the handle is struck at the top
with a rawhide mallet to drive the point

FORMED MODULAR POT *(detail)*. Larry
Jones. Formed leather with a frank use
of lacing that holds the parts together
and incorporates strips of leather brought
up from section below.

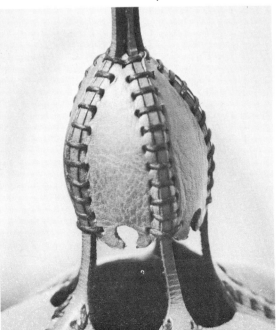

into the leather. Always back the piece you are working on with wood or other material to protect the cutting end of the tool as it penetrates the leather.

Thonging chisels may be purchased that have one to eight prongs. Cutting ends of prongs may make a round, straight, or diagonal split. The length of individual prongs ranges from $\frac{3}{32}$ of an inch to $\frac{1}{8}$ of an inch cut.

When using thonging chisels, it is helpful to have a straight line indicated along the edge to be stitched. If the stitch is to be sewn above the surface, draw a line the desired distance from the edge with a fork tine, caliper, ruler and pencil, or an edge

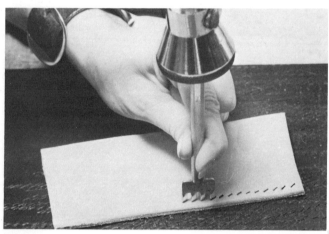

A thonging chisel with 45° prongs is held firmly against the grain side of a dry piece of leather and struck with a rawhide, wood, or craftsman's weighted mallet *(shown here)*, having hickory and lignum vitae striking surfaces.

Many processes shown in the following pages are worked with wet leather. There is sometimes a tendency to rush a job and make thonging slits before the leather dries. However, when the chisel is pulled from wet leather, it will tend to stretch the leather permanently *(rear)*. The chisel driven through dry leather will result in a neat end product *(front)*.

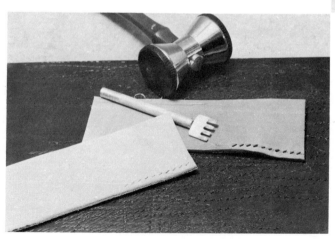

Placing stitches evenly from an edge is facilitated by making a guideline with a fork tine or measuring with a ruler and impressing a line with a stylus or an awl.

beveler (see page 34). However, if you wish the stitching to be below the surface of the leather, you should cut a grooved line with an edge groover. Sinking the stitch protects the thread or lacing from ordinary wear.

Additional tools used for stitching include a spacer for marking stitching holes evenly and an overstitcher. The overstitcher pushes the finished stitch down into the groove. Awls and awl hafts are handy for making holes and spreading slits. A stitching pony is shown.

The different needles and methods required for sewing thread and lace are illustrated on the following pages.

A stitching groover is used when you wish to countersink the thread or lacing below the surface of the leather. It actually cuts a groove with a sharp cutting point at the end of an adjustable L-shape projection. Adjustability allows you to move your stitching groove from 1/16 to 3/4 inch from the edge. The cut line feeds out through a tiny hole above the cutting blade, which may be pushed or pulled along the leather's edge. The adjustable gouge *(page 47)* also may be used for this process.

To keep slits evenly spaced, make a first punch along the premarked line. Then, place the first prong of the chisel in the last hole of the preceding set of slits. With each new punch, there will be one less slit than the total number of prongs.

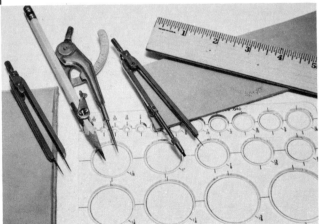

Other convenient tools for measuring distances from edges or making circles are calipers, a compass, and craftsman's tools. A plastic template for determining hole sizes, angles, and curves also may be employed. With this template you can accurately measure distances between holes and determine hole placement before punching.

STITCHING AND LACING

Stitching and lacing are used primarily for holding two pieces of leather together. Because stitching and lacing usually are decorative as well as functional, both of these techniques are carefully planned. Whether you use thread stitching or the wider leather lacing depends on the project and your individual taste. The conventional cowboy lacing styles have been adapted by artists and craftsmen in their new approaches to leather, but less obviously. The saddle stitch is still valid for line and edging stitches, but it also works toward the total appearance of a piece in addition to its practicality.

Stitching materials include several types of threads in black, white, or bone. Prewaxed linen thread is easily sewn through the thonged slits. Carpet thread, unwaxed linen, cotton, Dacron, and silk thread also may be used for sewing leather. To wax thread, pull it along a piece of beeswax; rewax it frequently as you sew. Any sewing counter or leather shop has beeswax. Dental floss also may be used for sewing leather. Slits and holes in the leather may have to be forced open with an awl or fid.

Lacing is wider than thread and is available in various colors and materials such as calf, goat, latigo, rawhide, and vinyl. Lacing comes in $\frac{3}{32}$-inch and $\frac{1}{8}$-inch widths and is sold by the spool, yard, or piece. Lacing is round or flat.

Thin leathers such as suede may be sewn on a sewing machine. If the action of a home machine stretches the bottom layer, lightly glue the seam allowance with rubber cement before sewing. Then, after sewing, open the seam and crease back. Gluing also may facilitate some hand sewing operations. Needle holes punched by an unthreaded sewing machine also serve as an excellent guide for hand stitching.

Hand sewing needs include waxed and unwaxed thread in lengths and spools, assorted needles, saddle stitching awl with removable bobbin, stitching awls, and beeswax. The leather object here illustrates a saddle stitched edge.

For stitching regularity, a spacing wheel designates even spacing of stitching holes, which will be made with an awl. The wheel turns and marks holes with its protrusion. The spacing wheel is made in three sizes: 5, 6, or 7 holes per inch. At rear is the overstitcher, a star-like wheel that is run over the finished stitch to push the thread into a grooved leather edge.

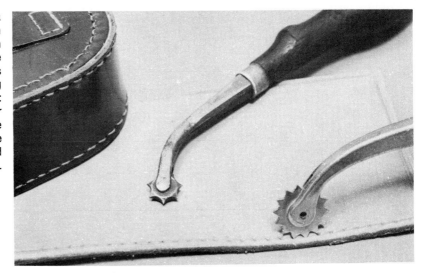

Stitching holes are made with an awl, which may have a round, tricornered, or curved blade. The awl is placed over the marked hole and tapped with a hammer in the same way as a punch. It also may be used to enlarge holes and to push a thread through a hole. A fid has a triangular blade and is used to enlarge holes for wider lacing. It may also be put under a lace to help tighten it as you sew. The pliers is used to pull or push needles and awls through the leather.

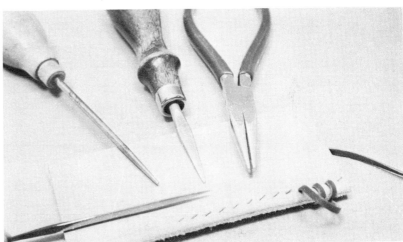

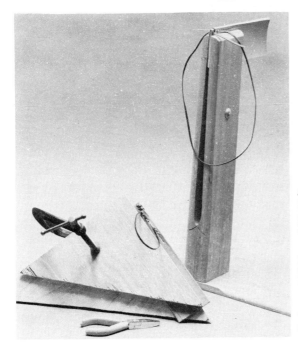

A stitching pony is often necessary to hold leather while you use both hands for sewing and pulling. The pony *(right)* is straddled, and your weight holds it down while the leather, clamped in the pony's jaws, is sewn. Improvise a pony by placing the leather between two pieces of wood held together with a C clamp or a vise. A larger "stitching horse," which resembles a cobbler's bench, also may be built; the C clamp is then attached to the seat, resembling the neck of a horse.

Sewing needles include a glover's needle *(top)* and different size harness needles *(bottom)* with curved triangular points and conventional but large eyes. You can see why it would be necessary to spread or enlarge a slit with an awl or fid to use these needles.

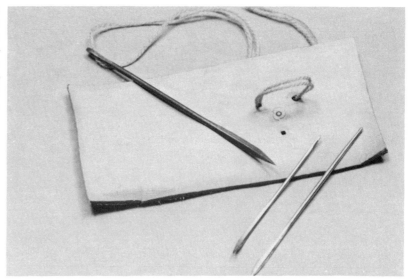

For lacing, special needles have single or double prongs and gripping teeth. The lace end should be skived and tapered to fit within the edges of the needle prongs.

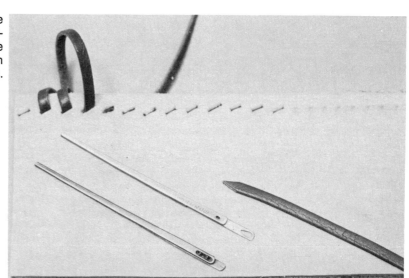

A life eye needle, made straight or curved, is handy for sewing around corners and tight spaces. The holding end of these needles has an interior threaded tube that grips the thread as it is turned. It may be used for round or flat lacing, which must be tapered to fit the needle hole. If the lace breaks and lodges in the tube, the flame from a lighted match held to the end will melt out the broken piece of lacing.

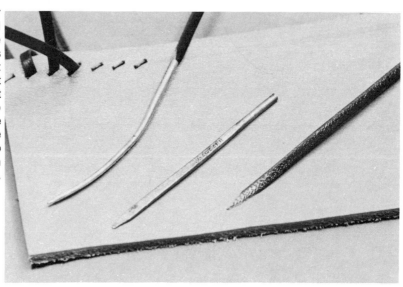

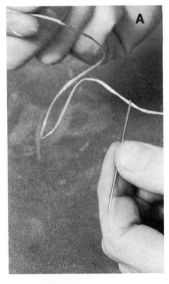

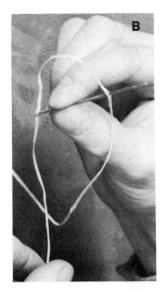

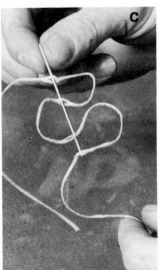

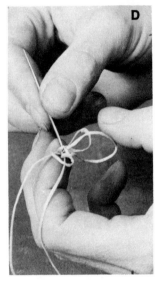

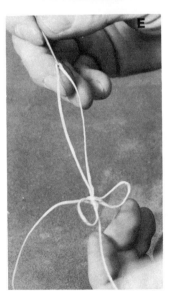

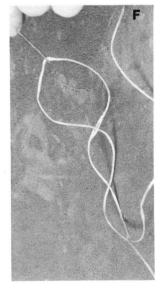

Saddle Stitching

Many sculptures, formed pots, and accessories are assembled with the saddle stitch, a sewing technique in which two needles are used simultaneously, one at each end of the thread. Each needle is pulled through a hole from each side, thereby placing a stitch on both sides of the leather and filling in the space between every hole on each side with thread. (A single running stitch only fills in the space between every other hole.) Because a needle is placed on each end of the thread, there is a trick to threading the needles so they won't slip.

A. Use a waxed linen thread and pull it through the eye of a harness needle, allowing about a 3-inch lead.
B. Poke the point of the needle back through the leader part of the thread, making a loop over your fingers.
C. Make two additional loops, then poke the needle through the thread two more times as shown.
D. After you have the loops threaded on the needle, slide them down over the eye end of the needle.
E. Pull the loops past the eye back down onto the main thread.
F. Pull the loops further and you have a thread that will not pull out of the needle as you work. Follow this procedure with both needles on the ends of the thread.

Should the natural twist of the thread open as you sew, twirl the needle between thumb and forefinger after every stitch to replace the lost twist. Be sure to begin with a long enough piece of thread so you don't have too many beginnings and endings in your stitching.

To begin the saddle stitch, pass one needle through the first hole and pull it through until the thread is equal on each side of the leather. Then pass both needles through the second hole at the same time but in opposite directions. Continue stitching each hole in this manner for the length of the seam. To end, lock the thread under the last stitch.

COVERED LEATHER BOTTLE.
Lacing is functional and
frankly decorative.

PHOTOGRAPHED AT KROCH'S &
BRENTANO'S, SKOKIE, ILL.

STUFFED SCULPTURE. Fred Borcherdt. Saddle stitching
results in a trim finished seam along the entire edge
as opposed to the running stitch, used for the belt
on page 41, in which the space between every other hole
is open. Both saddle and running stitches are used as
a straight edge line in contrast to a stitch that covers the
edge, as in the hat on page 41.

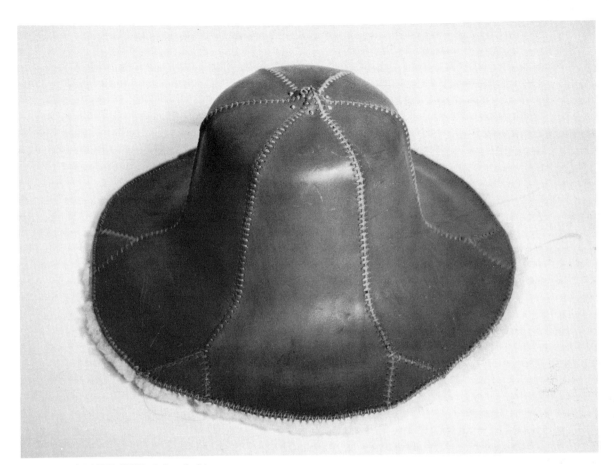

FORMED HAT. John Snidecor. Carefully spaced threads are used to join the formed part of the hat and to cover the edges. An extra piece of lacing is laid across and stitched with the seam for extra detailing. A double whip stitch is used at the brim edge to finish the hat and hold the fur lining in place.

COURTESY, ARTIST

BELT. Robert Zyer. A running stitch may be used along an edge, in the center, anywhere for any reason.

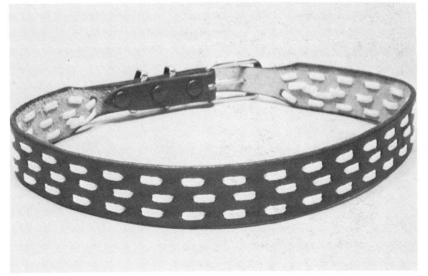

VARIOUS IDEAS FOR STITCHING AND LACING

Wide, bold cross, and angled lacing contribute to this design. Don Edwards

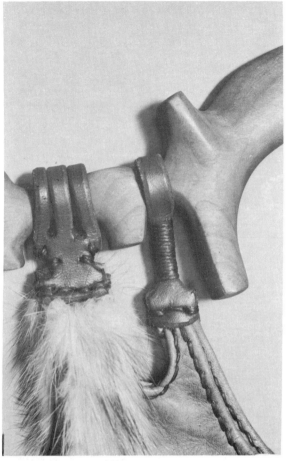

Saddle stitching and wrapping are used on this detail from a pouch on page 91.
John Cederquist

A lace of leather is placed along the seam and stitched in for an added raised detail.
(See pot, page 88.)
John Cederquist

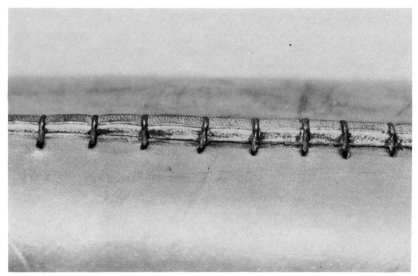

Stitches more often associated with needlework are used to exaggerate the seams of a suede-covered octagonal box. Joy Lobell

Machine stitching is used decoratively. Bruce Vetter

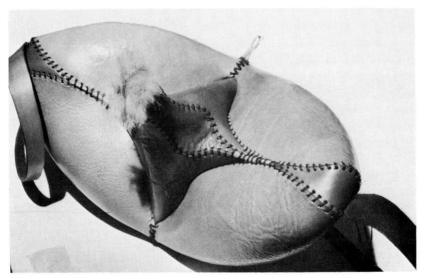

The whip stitch is used to hold together modular forms of different materials and to add to the decorative treatment.

PHOTOGRAPHED AT DESIGN WEST, LOS ANGELES

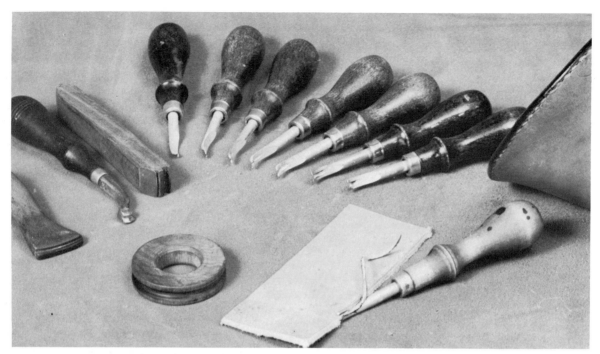

Tools for edge finishing *(clockwise from front)* are a round edge
slicker and straight edge slicker; metal and wood edge creaser;
a series of different size edge bevelers for varying thicknesses of
leather. A rounded and dyed edge shows a finished stitch.
Foreground: an edge beveler removes sharp corner from flesh side
of leather.

FINISHING EDGES

Edges of cut leather present a finished appearance when they are rounded, beveled, smoothed, or burnished. You usually finish the edges that will show, such as the edges of a belt, the flap of a handbag, or the seam of a sculpture. Tools for rounding and beveling vary in size for use with different thicknesses of leather. These tools are an edge beveler, an edge creaser, and a burnisher. For a final touch, edges may be dyed the same or contrasting color (see the section on coloring in this chapter).

Edges may be finished when leather
is dry or "cased," meaning dampened.
Leather is dampened lightly by
rubbing it with a wet sponge on both
sides. Allow leather to dry about five
minutes and to return to almost
original color; then work it. Edges
usually smooth better when they are
dampened with water or rubbed with
beeswax to seal and burnish them.

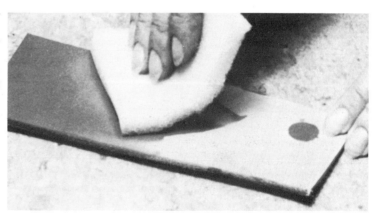

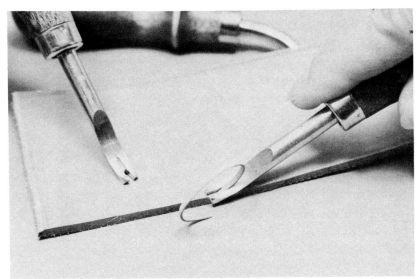

The edge beveler may be used on the grain, flesh, or both sides of the leather. Push the tool along the edge, producing a uniform cut. The spaces between prongs of the edge beveler vary and are indicated by numbers 1 (very narrow) to 5 (quite wide) for different thicknesses of leather. When cutting, hold the tool with the prongs curved upward at about a 30° angle to the leather. You can go over an edge a couple of times. The cutting edge between the prongs may be sharpened with a small round jeweler's file or stropped by pulling a heavy cord dipped in jeweler's rouge along the cutting edge at the back of the curve.

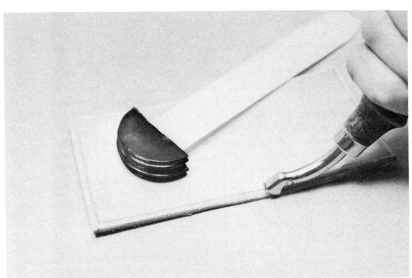

For an extra detail, a single, double, or triple line may be placed parallel to the edge using an edge creaser. This tool has a long flange, which is placed at the edge of the leather to serve as a guide. A shorter flange embosses a straight line as the tool is pulled along the dampened leather edge. Widths between flanges vary; if a double or triple line is desired, use three different width edge creasers. An edge cutter has a similar appearance and size range as the creaser; the difference is that the short flange is sharp and actually cuts a line from the leather rather than embosses it.

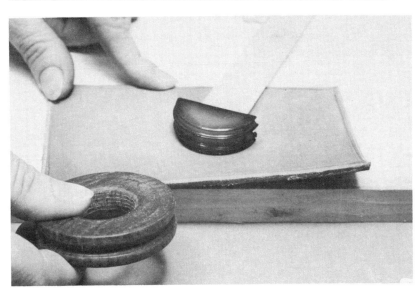

Burnishing is accomplished by rubbing the leather edge back and forth with a grooved edge slicker. Project the leather edge to be burnished over your cutting board just enough to allow back and forth movement of the tool. If the edge is slightly wet or rubbed with wax, the pores will round off and close more easily. A wooden circle slicker is shown in use. The end of the plastic tool *(rear)* has three grooves designed to fit different leather thicknesses. This is called a 3-in-1 bone creaser. The flat arm of the bone creaser is used for flattening seams, and the end point is for creasing.

BENDING, FOLDING, CREASING

Many projects require a bend, fold, or crease in the leather. One or more of these operations usually apply when making sculptures, boxes, purses, straps, seams, and other objects. It is important that the bend, crease, or fold be permanently set so the leather will not spring back to its original position.

For thicker leather, over 4 to 5 ounces, it is necessary to cut a U- or V-shaped groove in the flesh side where you wish the bend to occur. Cut the groove with a stitching groover, wood-cutting chisel, or adjustable leather-grooving tool. Case the leather with a wet sponge, especially at the bend, then bend. Devise a way to hold the leather to the desired bend until it dries. Always allow extra leather length in your project when bends are planned. Use vegetable-tanned leathers whenever you intend to fold or form.

For thin leathers, under 3 ounces, you usually can crease the leather by folding it back on itself. Then, tap or pound the fold with a mallet or rub it with the flat arm of the bone creaser. If necessary, dampen the leather on the flesh side at the line of the fold. Gluing a fold will help hold it in place. After gluing, smooth the leather so there are no wrinkles and place a heavy object, such as a book, on it.

SOFT SCULPTURE. Fred Borcherdt. 12 in. high. This piece shows an application of folded leather for sculpture. Vegetable-tanned leather was wet (saturated as in Chapter 4) and crushed to the desired shape; then it was weighted until dry. Seams are saddle stitched; edges are beveled and burnished.

The adjustable gouge is used to make a groove in the leather so it will fold readily. The depth of the cutting blade is adjusted by twisting the handle; it works much like the blade of a woodworking plane. Try to keep grooves as shallow as possible so as not to weaken the leather. The gouge also may be used for grooving before stitching.

Fold the leather along the groove. Unless a groove is made, you can only achieve a rounded corner by folding. A groove is essential for achieving a 35° or greater bend because it eliminates a length of the flesh along the bend line. Experiment with depth of gouge needed, using a piece of scrap leather before working an entire project. Be careful not to go so deep that you mar the grain side of the leather.

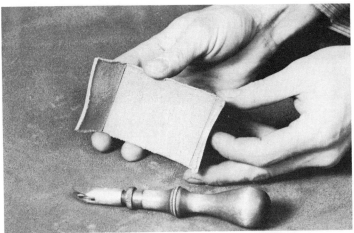

Folds, depending upon the thickness of the leather, may require dampening, then pressing with a mallet against a hard surface. A marble slab or a lithograph stone is a good surface for efficient seam pounding and pressing.

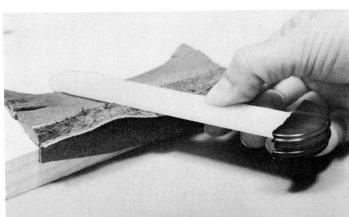

For pressing lighter weight leathers, the versatile bone creaser has a long, flat end that is rubbed back and forth across the fold. Any smooth tool may be used as long as it does the job.

The ability to bend and shape wet leather is illustrated by these delightful animals. Using the pattern below, thoroughly wet a 5- to 6-ounce vegetable-tanned leather by dipping it in water and shaping it by hand. Rounded bends do not require gouging, but riveted spots must be skived. Riveting is done at the nose, elbows, and under the back legs. Transfer the pattern to tracing paper; enlarge if desired. Cut the leather out from the pattern and mark dotted line (indicated on pattern) on the underside of the leather with a pencil. Fold leather along dotted lines. Rivet at points of matching letters. Skive all corners to be riveted under the back legs. Numbers 1, 2, 3, 4, 5 should be riveted to A.

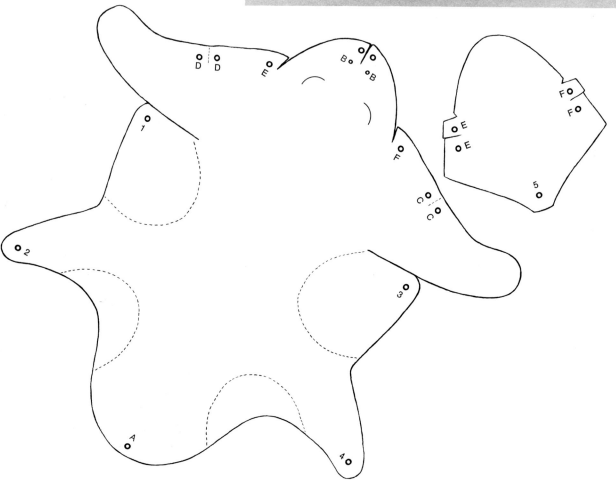

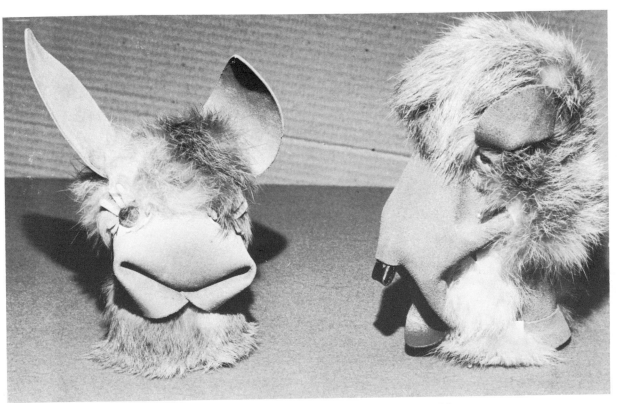

Several combinations of folds can result in an entire menagerie. Combine two or more pieces of leather for ears, feet, base, etc. For eyes use scraps, rivets, or plastic eyes available at craft shops. To begin, wet a piece of leather and play with it until the folds suggest the form. The imaginative designing is up to you.

PHOTOGRAPHED AT KROCH'S & BRENTANO'S, SKOKIE, ILL.

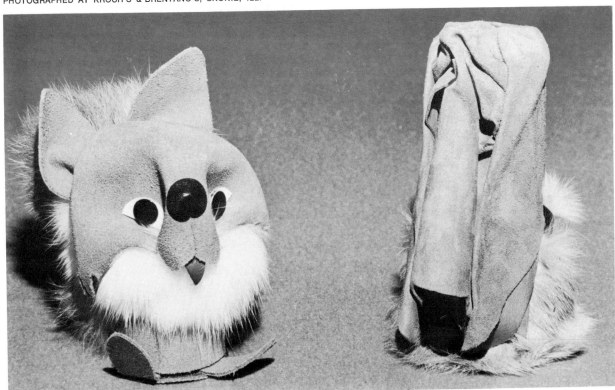

LEATHER CHEST WITH MIRRORS. Joy Lobell.
11 in. high, 14 in. wide, 14 in. deep. Bending
suede and leather around corners is a widely
used technique. For sharper corners, the
flesh side should be skived or lightly grooved.
In this chest suede is pulled tightly around
corners, and the edges of the wood box are
trimmed with mink. Mirrors and brass
hardware are added.

COURTESY, ARTIST

The interior of the box above has a fabric lining
worked around pieces of cardboard cut to fit
the inside. The suede outside covering must be
thoroughly creased and smoothed to adhere
to the inside of the box.

TOOLING AND CARVING

Most often, decorative leatherwork is associated with traditional, intricately stamped designs. Traditionally, stamping, carving, and embossing in the United States have been done in the Western style. You've no doubt seen this style in flowers, animals, borders, and a combination of patterns used on saddles, wallets, belts, purses, and suitcases.

Contemporary artists experimenting with new approaches to leather are using stamping and carving in unique ways and are producing results totally different from the Western style. These artists may employ regular carving tools, but they apply them to contemporary designs. They even may use non-traditional methods to evolve an entirely new approach to the tooling-carving idea.

There are, literally, scores of books on how to tool leather in the traditional manner. For our purposes, however, tools will be introduced and examples offered in a way that will stimulate another artistic statement. This discussion does not denigrate traditional designs, for which we have the greatest admiration, but rather, in keeping with the scope of the book, attempts to make the reader aware of other approaches.

TRADITIONAL TOOLING is artistically executed in this intricately designed saddle detail from Mexico. Leather is modeled, embossed, lined, stippled, stamped, and carved. The artistry, technique, patience, and talent required for this type of work are infinite.

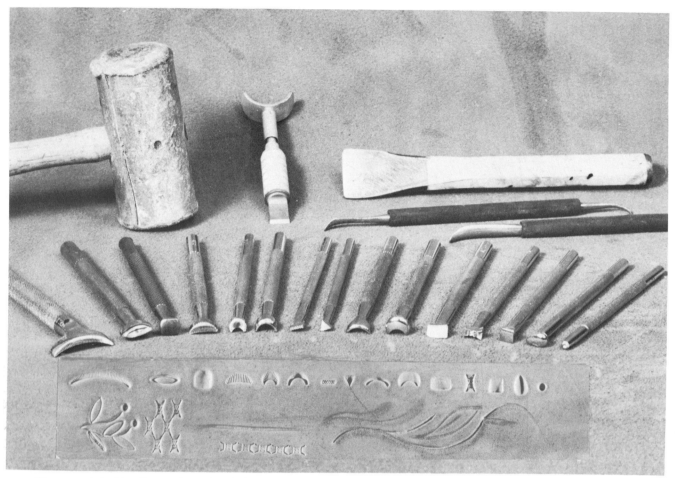

Chrome-plated tooling and carving instruments include *(rear)* rawhide hammer, swivel knife with interchangeable blades, cold chisel with cutting edge rounded and polished for tooling a groove, and two rounded-bowl modeling tools. An assortment of stamping tools *(front)* with designs on the base for impressing into wet leather is useful. *At bottom,* the designs made with these stamps are illustrated.

Tooling involves stamping into damp leather to create raised and impressed designs. Although there are scores of stamping-tool heads, you can do a multitude of things with only a few—even with only the point of an aluminum nail, the bowl of a spoon, the tine of a fork, wax-modeling and wood-carving tools, and discarded dental instruments.

Cased, full-grain, vegetable-tanned leather (also called oak-tanned leather) is recommended for tooling. Case the leather by rubbing a moist sponge over it (as shown previously), first on the grain side and then the flesh side. When the moisture begins to dry and the original color returns, the cased leather is ready for tooling. If the leather is too wet, the tooled impressions will close up; if it is too dry, it will be hard to pull a tool across the surface to yield a line. If the leather dries as you work, simply remoisten it by wiping a damp sponge across the entire piece.

When using improvised tools, be sure they are chrome-plated, brass, stainless steel, or aluminum so they won't rust and

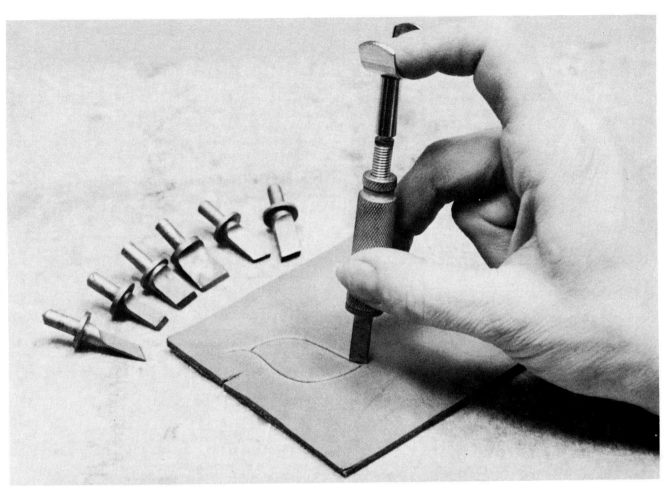

The swivel knife is a versatile tool for creating lines in leather. It is held as shown. The index finger on the saddle top exerts pressure; the wrist is supported on the table. The forefinger and thumb, placed near the bottom of the swivel, control the direction of the blade to achieve curves and reverse lines without lifting the tool from the surface. Angles of blades on interchangeable bits yield different line sizes and slants. Blades may be sharpened by drawing them across a whetstone.

leave a stain on the leather. Water containers for sponges should be made of glass, plastic, or stainless steel, because any time wet leather is in contact with certain metals, they will tend to leave a stain on the leather. Of course, water containers should be kept clean.

In tooling, tools are either pulled across the leather surface with the hand to make lines or are hit with a mallet to make a series of dents and shapes. (As with punches, use only a rawhide or wood mallet, not a metal one, so you don't destroy the end of the tool.) Hold the mallet loosely in one hand. Hold the tool down near the head with the other hand and rest the wrist on the table to support the tool and direct it more accurately. Tool leather on a marble or lithograph stone that is perfectly smooth to protect the tool and to provide a smooth surface.

Today, artists and craftsmen have been combining leather tooling with carving, embossing, and painting, among other techniques, in the hope of achieving unique and interesting forms.

FRAGMENT OF A WALL COVERING. Holland. 1680. Leather stamped, embossed, painted, and varnished has a stylized, almost abstract design in contrast to traditional Western tooling.

COLLECTION, COOPER-HEWITT MUSEUM OF DECORATIVE ARTS AND DESIGN, SMITHSONIAN INSTITUTION

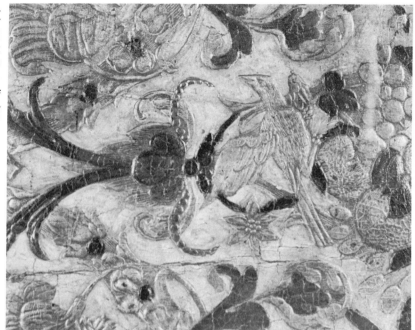

COMPOSITION NO. 3. Julian Martin de Vidales. 1970. Tooled leather mural.

COURTESY, GALERIA JUANA MORDO, MADRID

FORMS AND SPACES. Julian Martin de Vidales. 3 ft. high,
2 ft. wide. COURTESY, GALERIA JUANA MORDO, MADRID

FINDINGS—DECORATIVE AND FUNCTIONAL

It used to be that findings, or hardware, for leather were used primarily for functional purposes: buckles to hold straps, rivets for holding pieces together, snaps for fastening, and grommets for lacing. Not so today. In addition to functional uses, findings are greatly design oriented. Along with manufactured findings, found objects such as buckles that once closed mailbags, cleats from masts, and fittings from bridles and saddles are being used imaginatively in a new context. Fastenings that might be thought of as both functional and decorative include rivets, snaps, eyelets, and grommets.

Rivets are metal fastening pins that are placed through a prepunched hole. A two-part rivet has a shaft and a cap; one piece is placed on each side of the leather and is closed by using a special setter that is hit with a metal hammer. A split rivet resembles a paper fastener that has a head and two prongs that are spread apart manually.

Snaps come in four parts; two for the cap and two for the eye. A snap setter consists of a plate to hold the base of each part and a tubelike cupped anvil that fits over the cap to keep it from being smashed when hit by the hammer.

Eyelets and grommets are metal linings that fit into the holes prepared for lacing and decoration. An eyelet is a one-piece tu-

Assorted rivets and their setting tools. Each size rivet requires its own setter. Each setter has a concave tube that fits over the rivet head and is hit with the hammer when setting. A direct hit on the curved rivet head without using a setter will flatten it; but some craftsmen prefer this to the rounded head look. At front, a rivet base poked through a punched hole in the leather is shown. The top will be inverted on the base and hit to set with a metal shoe hammer. At left, the set rivet is shown.

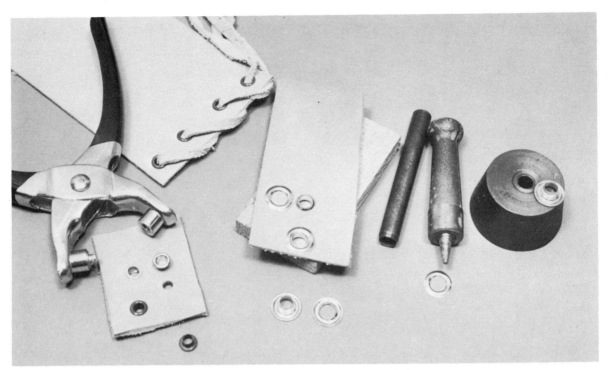

Eyelet punch and setter *(left)*. This pliers-like tool will first punch a hole in the leather, then squeeze the two parts of the eyelet together so the base and top are permanently crimped. Heavier duty eyelet punches and setters are required for thicker leather. Or use the revolving punch to make the hole, then set the eyelet with a tool. A grommet *(right)* is a two-part hole liner, having a top and a ring. A special grommet setter *(right)* is required. It has a base with a hole and a long tube, which is inserted in the hole to set the grommet.

bular shaft with a head that is mashed into the leather with a special eyelet setter that secures it. A grommet is a two-part liner having a head and a ring. One part is placed on each side of the leather and both are joined by using a grommet setter and a hammer.

Rivets, snaps, eyelets, and grommets are available in various sizes, shapes—round, oval, square—and in a variety of metallic and paint finishes. Each package of findings usually contains a setter and directions for use. A wide assortment of buttons, buckles, cleats, and other decorative fastenings may be obtained from saddleries, shoemaker and leather shops and suppliers, hardware stores, sewing counters, and jewelry findings companies.

With a pressure riveter simply place the rivets where desired and pull the handle toward you to exert pressure on the rivet.

Assorted findings for fastening and decorating leather include those that pierce the leather and are bent on the left side plus some that may be glued.

In addition to manufactured buckles and improvised closings, many craftsmen create their own designs from forged, welded metals.

Various diameters of silver buttons and spots are used decoratively on the front of a belt designed by Frank Stephens.

PHOTOGRAPHED AT
ULTIMO, CHICAGO

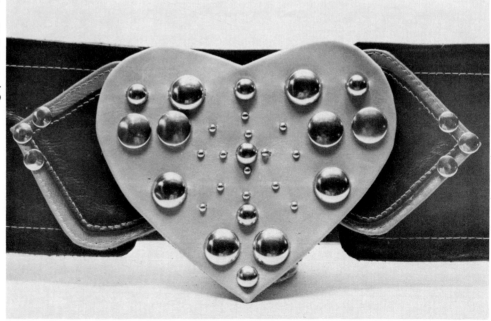

Snaps, rivets, and buckles do more than provide a fastening for leather in strategic places. They are carefully placed to create a visual rhythm. By Truman Xavier Jones

Brass eyelets and findings create the total surface decoration of this purse.

PHOTOGRAPHED AT ULTIMO, CHICAGO

Grommets are used for oversize holes for lacing this belt designed by Bruce Vetter.

COLORING AND FINISHING

Traditionally, leather has been colored with dyes that penetrate the pores of the material. Recent experimentation now includes many other coloring materials more often associated with art media. These include artists' oils and acrylics, household dyes for tie-dyeing, batik dyes for the wax-resist process, pen and ink, and felt-tip markers. Although many of these methods still fall into the category of experimental, many of the fine results underscore the validity of trying new approaches to leather coloring.

Because of the unpredictability of the material and existing tannery dye processes, coloring leather can either be a tremendously successful endeavor or a highly frustrating one. Because each skin is different in porosity and texture, each piece of leather accepts coloring in a different way. What may work well on one piece of leather could be a dismal blotch on another. With this in mind, let's discuss usual and innovative methods for coloring and finishing leather.

Leather may be easily stained with almost any liquid—coffee, coke, even water. If you accidentally spill a staining liquid on a piece of leather, you usually are advised to stain the entire piece with the same liquid so it will be the same color overall rather than spotted. One color may be covered with another or antiqued with a special leather antiquing color for unusual appearance.

Probably the first planned coloring you will try will be edge dyeing; then you'll try piece dyeing and possibly even whole skin dyeing.

Edge dyeing means that you color the edges of a leather project such as a belt or sculpture (before or after burnishing) with a matching or contrasting color.

In piece dyeing you apply color to the surfaces of certain pieces of leather to be used in a project before the parts are assembled. If you do the dyeing after the project is assembled, stitches and seams may not dye evenly. Always complete the dyeing before adding hardware to your project.

To dye a whole skin, brush or spray on the dye solution over the entire hide before cutting, punching, or tooling, so you begin a project with a relatively even color over the entire piece of leather.

Dyes

Chemicals for coloring, such as Fiebing's and Omega dyes, usually are composed of a mineral oil and spirit solution. Aniline dyes have either a water or alcohol base; solvents for these are usually stated on the labels. Recently, however, some companies have been keeping their die solvents a mystery. But a letter to the company asking for a chemical breakdown will give you a clue as to what you can use to thin down their product.

Dyes are used in liquid form to penetrate the pores of wet or dry leather. On wet leather dye soaks in readily, resulting in a deep tone; on dry leather the pores are not as receptive to coloring and the tone is softer.

Dyes may be applied to edges with daubers, pipe cleaners, or Q-tips. For piece and whole-skin dyeing wipe on the dye with a sponge, cloth, cotton, wick material, brush, or spray. Applicators used with oil and spirit dyes are cleaned by rinsing them in a turpentine solvent and then washing them in soap and water. Applicators used with water-soluble dyes are cleaned with plain water.

For leatherworkers who use large quantities of dye, some dyes are sold as dry powder and are prepared by mixing with the required water, alcohol, or mineral oil

VEST. Linda Vetter. Brown dyed garment leather is designed and painted with Testor's Craft paints. It is approached much as an artist uses canvas.

BARRETTES. Linda Vetter. Cowhide first is dyed with leather dyes for overall background color, which is then embellished with craft paints for design.

and spirit solvents. Large quantity powder dyes usually are more economical than premixed dyes, and the colors are easy to control by adding more or less of the solvent to the powder. Aniline dyes, used for wood, also can be used for leather with excellent results. Many craftsmen who use aniline dyes prefer to work with vegetable-tanned, unfinished, unglazed, natural skins that have not been previously colored at the tannery.

Both the grain and flesh sides of leather may be dyed. However, because of the differences in texture and porosity, the color may not have the same tone on each side. Always experiment on scraps before you

begin. Lacing, too, may be dyed to match or to contrast with a project. If lacing stiffens, rub it with saddle soap, Lexol, or Vaseline to relubricate it, but wipe off the excess before using the laces.

Frequently, a first coat of dye will leave spots and blotches after drying because of an uneven penetration of color into the pores. Go over the project two or three times if necessary.

For maximum color control, apply dyes liberally with long back and forth or circular overlapping strokes. Any tinting, shading, or a multitude of other color effects may be added to a piece with brushes or daubers.

Leather dyes are available in both liquid and powdered aniline stains. Some normally are sold in a powder form for use on wood. Aniline stain powders must be mixed with water, alcohol, turpentine, or other solvents as directed. Jars *(right)* are improvised containers for keeping small amounts handy. They have wicks made of hardware store thresholding felt rolled up and placed in a cover *(center)*. By keeping the rolled wick in the cover with a length in the dye, the dye is evenly distributed on the applicator, and it is ready for use. A snap grip surgical scissors holds disposable cotton balls for edge dyeing.

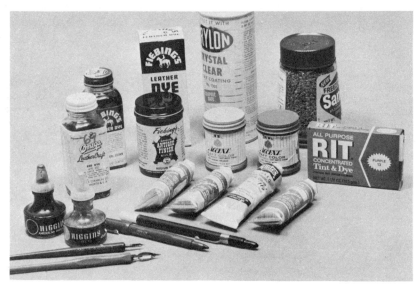

Assorted coloring materials applicable to leather include: leather dyes, antique finish, household dyes, inks, oil and acrylic paints, spray finishes, and felt tip pens.

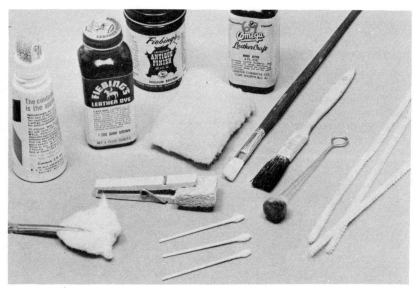

Applicators for dyes may be improvised from many materials or purchased ready to use. These include daubers, paint brushes, pens, sponge held in a clothespin, cotton balls in a hair clip, padded cloth, pipe cleaners, and Q-tips. For spraying dyes use a spray gun or air brush.

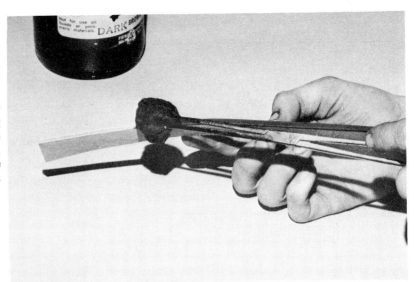

Edge dyeing with a small dauber and long-handled instrument makes dipping the dauber into dye easy. Blot off excess dye, then pull dauber along edge of leather.

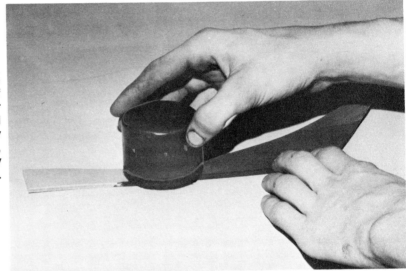

Project dyeing may include dyeing grain and flesh sides of parts of the project before or after assembly. Here, the rolled wick in the cover of a spray serves as a broad dauber surface, which is loaded evenly with coloring.

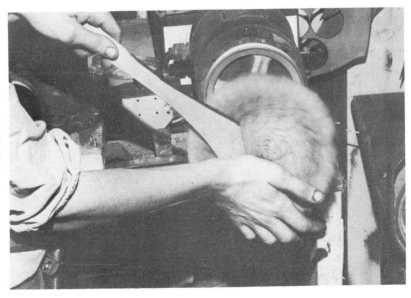

Buff the leather with a soft cloth, by hand, after saddle soap or other finishes are applied. Leather can be treated much like wood. After applying a floor paste wax to the leather, buff it on an electrically operated sheepskin buffing wheel.

Preparation for Dyeing

Always clean the leather surface to be dyed to remove dust, leather particles, and any cement left from gluing. There are prepared leather cleaners, or mix your own by using one teaspoon of oxalic acid (from the drug store) with one pint of water. Always cover your work surface with clean paper, not newspaper. Keep other dyes out of the way, and wear disposable plastic or rubber gloves. Dab your applicator on a waste piece of leather instead of applying directly to the skin in order to avoid a build-up of color each time you apply new dye.

COLLAGE. Ruben Steinberg. Applications of various colors and shades of acrylics, some thinned with water so they have a dribbling effect, are used in a painterly manner.

Mixing Colors

Feel free to mix colors and build up one color over another for special effects. Fiebing's Chemical Company has a color chart with twenty-four colors plus gray, black, and white. They recommend stripping off the tanning finish with "Dye-Prep" to make the leather more receptive to dyes. Also, when changing from a previously dyed color, it is best to do it in two steps. First, neutralize the original color with an intermediate color. Then repeat the dyeing process with your final color. For example, to dye:

> White leather black, dye it green or blue, then black;
> White to dark blue, first use weak black (4 to 1), then dark blue;
> White to brown, first dye light green, then brown;
> Red to black, first use green, then black;
> Green to black, first dye red, then black;
> White to bright red, first dye yellow, then red;
> White to dark red, first use tan, then dark red.

Always let the first color dry before applying the second.

Dyes may be combined to achieve intermediate colors or tones in the same way paints are mixed. Usually the basic color wheel combinations apply. For example:

> Yellow and blue = varying shades of green;
> Yellow and red = varying shades of orange to red;
> Red and blue = shades of deep purple to lavender;
> Red and purple = wine;
> Brown and yellow = golden brown or tan;
> Brown and red = maroon or dark brown.

An infinite number of color shades are possible. Mixtures can be tested on swatches until the desired color is achieved.

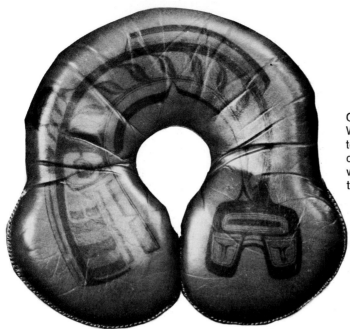

CHAIR CUSHION. Fred Borcherdt. Waterproof felt tip pens were used to recreate a Northwest Coast Indian design of a fish. Garment leather was shaped and stuffed with foam to make a desk chair cushion.

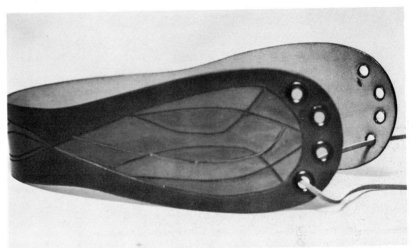

BELT. Murry Kusmin. Belt colored with leather dyes in a contemporary manner. Grooved shapes each contain a different color or hue.

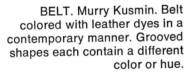

BELT. Bruce Vetter. Two pieces of colored leather have been combined; a purple dyed suede has been glued and sewn as a lining beneath the antique-toned cowhide with cutouts made on a clicker machine. Grommets are used for lacing.

LEATHER BATIK. Fred Borcherdt. The wax-resist process can result in original effects on leather. Pieces may be combined for any number of unusual projects: art statements, clothing, accessories, added details. Or batik leather pieces may be used simply as decorative hangings.

Other Coloring Media

Coloring methods and materials borrowed from other art forms are increasingly being applied to leather. Artists' oil paints may be painted or spread directly on leather. Or the leather may be sealed first with a plastic spray sealer or leather sealer to prevent oil from penetrating the skin. When the paint dries, another coat of plastic sealer will protect the surface against scratching and flaking. Acrylic paints (a water-base opaque medium) may be used right out of the tube or bottle or thinned with water for a more transparent toning.

Some acrylics may crack and brush off when dry, depending on both the product and the skin. If the leather is to be worn, the paint should be flexible when dry and not crack. For murals and collages, flexibility is not so important. Pen and ink and waterproof felt-tip pens also can be used successfully on leather. But with these, too, seal them after they have dried.

A contemporary method of coloring leather is the process of tie-dye or tie bleach. To begin, fold the leather into squares or bundles, and tie the folded leather tightly in two or three places with lacing material or waxed linen thread—anything that will not slip when wet. Dip the tied leather into a fabric- or leather-dye solution. The time it takes to penetrate the leather varies considerably depending upon its thickness, the number of folds, strength of the dye, and amount of time in the dye. Obviously, you should experiment considerably before beginning a project. However, the appeal of the tie-dye technique is simply that it is so unpredictable.

In tie bleaching, the leather should be tied up as in the tie-dye technique, then dipped into bleach to remove some of the existing color. This results in a tied pattern. Stones may be tied into the folds of the leather to stretch it and cause color absorption in unusual patterns. Bleached leather should be thoroughly rinsed.

Batik is a wax-resist dye process that can be used successfully on leather. Melt paraffin or beeswax and brush it on the leather wherever you do *not* wish color. Then dye the leather with any special batik dyes or leather dyes already discussed. After the dye dries, place newspaper or newsprint on top of the areas that are waxed. Then press a hot iron on the paper so the wax melts and is absorbed by the newspaper. You may have to repeat the ironing procedure several times to remove all the wax. Another effect is achieved by crushing the waxed leather to create cracks in the wax. Then, when dyeing the leather, the coloring will penetrate the cracks and result in an unusual hairline abstract design.

In all coloring processes, first experiment on scraps. Dye time, bleach time, strength of dyes, and rinsing time all are extremely variable.

Restoring Oils

Through dyeing, leathers lose much of their oils. After the leather has dried, replace the oils by dipping it into a bath of neat's-foot oil or rubbing it with saddle soap or other leather conditioner–restorers. The leather then may be waxed, polished, and buffed.

To tie-dye, gather the material neatly and tie with a sturdy twine that will not loosen when wet. Dip the leather in bleach to remove color or in dye to add color. The dye time and strength of dye vary and should be experimented with.

DRAWSTRING PURSE. Marty Eisenstadt. Suede was tie-dyed; then the parts were cut and sewn together.

Clear Lacquer Finishes

Craftsmen and artists whose pieces are exposed to weather and handling at art fairs and other display areas often put a clear finish on a piece to protect it. A clear lacquer, thinly wiped, sprayed, or brushed onto the piece will provide a protective coating over water-base dyes. Lacquer may be incompatible with oil dyes and tend to dissolve them. Again, experiment first and, if necessary, use a special primer before finishing a piece with lacquer. Plastic spray coatings may also be used to protect your work.

BONDING—GLUING

Almost anytime you want to put two or more pieces of leather together, you can bond them with cement or glue. The type of glue you select depends on how you are going to use the leather to be joined.

Gluing may be used alone for seams; or the seam may be glued first, then sewn for extra strength. Gluing is indispensable for collage and mural work, for adhering glue to wooden shapes, for building up layers of leather for sculpture, and for permanently bonding shoe soles.

Basically, there are two families of bonding agents. The first includes wet glues such as white emulsion glues (Elmer's, Sobo), rubber cement, hide glue, woodworking glues, and Testor's Duco Cement. These are called "wet" glues because the surfaces of the leather are placed together while the glue is wet, then pressure is applied to the parts until the glue dries. Normally, these glues are used when parts are not to be given a great deal of wear or exposure to weather and handling. Many wet glues are not waterproof. However, you can use them for collages and sculpture; for covering large surfaces with leather; and for bonding small scraps to be used for jewelry such as earrings, pendants, and bracelets. With wet glues, you can move and readjust the glued parts before the glue sets, correcting placement mistakes readily.

The second type of bonding agents are the "contact" cements such as Weldwood, Barge's, Masters, and Petronio. These cements are spread on each of the pieces to be joined and allowed to dry until tacky. Then the two pieces are pressed together. Adhesion occurs on "contact," so if you

REFUGEE POTS. Murry Kusmin. Several layers of leather circles are laminated by cementing to build up thickness that is normally unavailable in leather. The pots are carved, sanded, and finished, using techniques similar to those used in woodworking. For detailed instructions on pot laminating, see page 92.

NECKLACE, EARRINGS, RING. Murry Kusmin.
Each "jewel" is made from two pieces of leather
grooved to fit around a "string" of leather belting,
then is glued in place. The earring end, where
the hanger is placed, is skived for a close fit
to the ear. The ring is secured with a rivet.

KEY CHAINS. Murry Kusmin. Scraps of
leather are used to advantage. Each key plaque is
made from two pieces of leather glued together
with the chain finding riveted. Designs are carved
and colored. Edges are colored and burnished.

err in placing a piece, you cannot easily readjust it. In using contact cements always follow specific product directions. Keep containers closed when not in use because these cements dry out quickly.

Some of the aspects you should consider when gluing are the results you want to achieve. If your project is designed so the leather must bend, then the glue should be flexible; rubber cements and dry bonds fulfill this requirement. The same kind of consideration should be given to cleanup. When dry, contact cements can be rolled or brushed off the leather. Some of the wet glues, however, often are so thin and runny that they penetrate thin leather and leave a spot on the visible surface; they also may dry stiff, which makes them useless for a project requiring flexible leather.

Before bonding any leathers over 3 to 4 ounces, rough up the surfaces to be adhered, thereby allowing the glue to penetrate deeper into the texture of the leather for stronger bonding. Rough up the leather with a small cheese-grater-like tool, a wire brush, coarse sandpaper, or tip of an awl.

The beauty of bonding is that you can laminate or build up endless sizes and shapes with leather in the same way that you do with wood. Otherwise both leather and wood have size limitations. A piece of leather is no larger than the hide from which it was made, and a piece of wood is no larger than the tree of its origin. Laminating can overcome these limits, yielding sizes greater than the original and allowing the artist and craftsman freedom as to size and shape.

Fashion designer La Bruja-Nicole illustrates how easily leather jewelry can be made with only scissors and cement, suede or garment leather, and a few interesting decorations.

Materials include patterns made from wood or heavy cardboard, leather, scissors, cement, and ornaments. Double parts are used so that the piece is heavy and conceals ends of the ornaments and tie pieces.

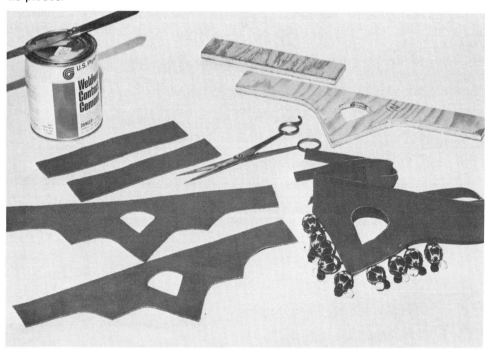

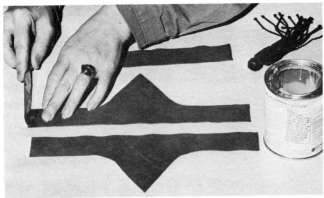

Cement is applied to each inside layer of the suede with a spatula (brushes tend to drip too easily). Contact cement must dry until tacky.

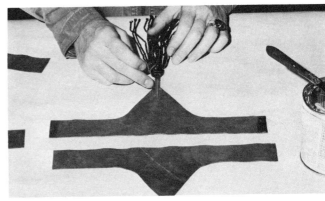

First the ornament is strung with a strip of leather and the leather placed at the bottom point of the neckpiece and cemented to the front layer.

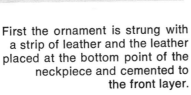

Ends are adhered. These will later be divided into four strips within a half inch of the solid band for easy tying at the back of the neck.

The lining piece is spread with cement. The tie is carefully placed and adhered. When using contact cements, remember that where you place a piece first is it.

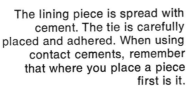

Before cementing ends of lining, be sure the tie parts lie flat over the inset piece. The tie will be cut into four strips, as shown in the photo at the top of page 70.

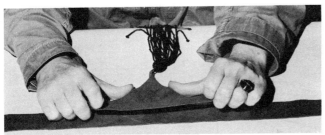

Cement lining to front and over the tie ends that will be cut into strips.

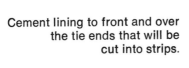

CHAPTER FOUR

Stretching and Forming

Antique hat blocks may be improvised as basic forms for a variety of shapes.

Among the remarkable properties of some leathers is that they assume a different personality when wet than dry. Vegetable-tanned leathers (also called oak tanned) are porous, and they absorb and hold water. While wet, leather can be stretched, molded, and shaped over a form. When it dries, the leather will be permanently contoured in its new shape until it is resaturated and reformed. You have no doubt had a leather shoe that was soaked by the rain. If the sole or top was bent when the leather was wet, the shoe would probably dry with the same bend. It is this stretching and forming quality of leather that enables manufacturers and craftsmen to mold it in an endless variety of shapes. The nose of a camera case is a good example of how leather can be stretched and formed to any shape.

The potential of leather forming is only beginning to be explored in an expressive, creative manner. Artists are using stretching and forming techniques to make hats, weed pots, bowls, trays, and coverings for myriad objects. They are stretching leather over armatures to make sculpture.

In the accompanying illustrations procedures for wetting, stretching, forming, and drying are shown and described in the captions. Once the new shape is dry, use the same techniques for joining, finishing, and decorating that are applicable to other types of leatherwork.

Block shapes used as forms for leather-molding can be hand carved or turned on a lathe. Use a soft porous wood, such as pine, that is easy to nail and will allow air to get to the underneath side of the leather so it will dry easily. For those who are hesitant about making their own wood forms, many suitable objects are available: the arm of an old chair or other broken furniture parts found in secondhand stores, whole or partial antique wood hat blocks used for shaping felt, and any other shape that presents itself to the imaginative eye.

Remember that wet leather reacts chemically with steel, so any nails used to pull and hold the leather taut should be galvanized or aluminum. Steel nails may cause wet leather to oxidize and stain; within hours the stained area will turn black. If you want streaks, however, you might purposely use steel nails.

The best leather for forming leather is 4- to 8-ounce vegetable-tanned cowhide. Shoulder and belly cuts are preferable over

HAND CARVED PINE HAT BLOCK AND
FINISHED HAT. John Snidecor. Leather has
been stretched over the block, and panels have
been cut and stitched with linen thread through
punched holes. The brim has been turned
under and rolled as it was formed. *(See following
demonstrations.)*

A two-part hat
block. Dome and
brim are formed
separately, then
stitched together.

side cuts because they have greater elasticity than side cuts. For testing the formability of a specific piece of leather, cut off a scrap, dip it in warm water, and fold it. If it holds the fold and is slippery feeling, it is most likely vegetable-tanned leather and can be used for forming. Chrome-tanned leather will spring back to its original shape after wetting and folding.

One- or multiple-piece forms may be used for forming leather, depending upon the shape desired. In this chapter hats formed over one and two piece shapes are illustrated. In the next chapter multi-pieced forms are shown for creating pots and boxes. Think in terms of combining one shape to another to make a whole, so that one mold can produce several identical shapes that may be combined. For variation you can rewet part of a piece of leather that has already been formed and mold that part into a different shape.

John Snidecor demonstrates his method for forming a three-part hat over a lathe-turned pine block that has been sanded smooth. First, the shape of leather is cut about 6 inches larger all around than the size of the block. This provides a rim for pulling, nailing, and trimming.

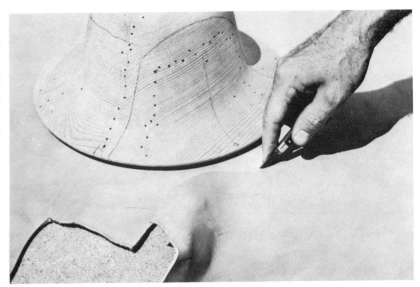

The leather is immersed in warm tap water for a few minutes until it is thoroughly wet. Ten minutes should be sufficient. A squirt of soap will help the water penetrate better. Excess water is gently squeezed out of the leather.

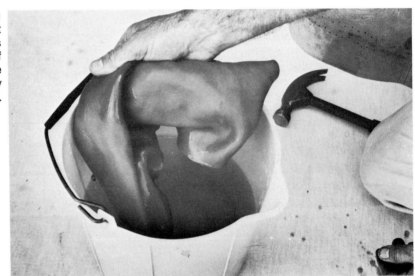

The wet leather is placed on the form and gently stretched and pulled to shape. Lines on the form indicate area over which each piece must be pulled.

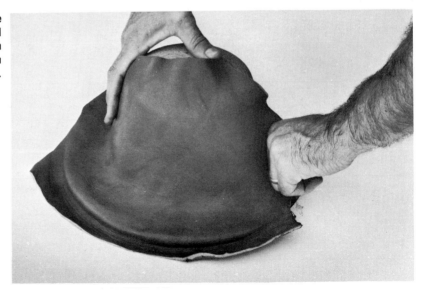

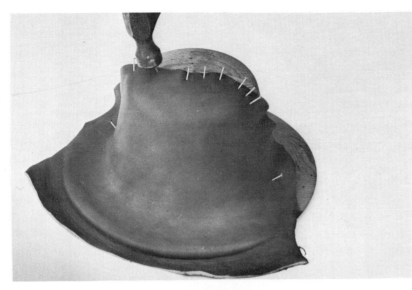

Nails are hammered through the leather into the block about ½ inch from edge of leather. Galvanized nails are used, and they are placed at an angle so the leather will not slide up. They are not hammered in all the way because it would be too hard to remove them.

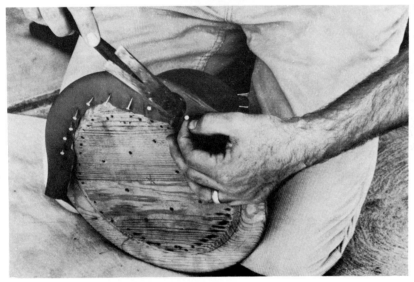

The leather is smoothed along the brim and nailed. Notice that the block is made from a solid piece of wood; it is not necessary to carve out the inside of the form.

The leather must dry thoroughly on the form for about 48 hours. When dry, panels are cut in the leather and the piece is removed from the block. Punching, lacing, coloring, and finishing follow. Some coloring may be done while the leather is wet. John Snidecor poses in the finished hat.

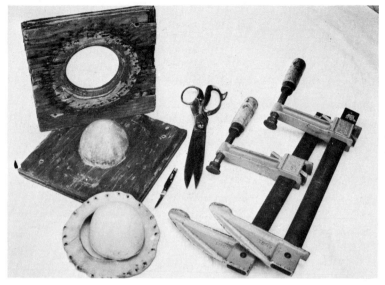

With a two-part frame, the crown and brim would be molded separately. The crown of this mold has been made from fiber glass. Plywood is used for the flat planes. Large C clamps are required to hold the part together. When the clamps are tightened, some water squeezes out of the leather so it can dry in the mold more quickly.

After the 6-ounce leather has been thoroughly wetted, it is formed and stretched over the bottom half of the mold. No nailing is necessary because the top half is placed over the dome, or crown, as shown, to hold it in place.

The two plywood forms are held together with four C clamps. Water begins to ooze from the leather almost immediately.

Bruce Vetter illustrates his method for making a two-piece hat consisting of crown and brim. The crown mold is an antique hat block; the brim is made from pine and plywood. First, wet leather is smoothed over the dome and held by nailing or by placing the brim shape over the leather edge. (Different height domes may be created with the brim shape.) For the brim, a hole is cut in the leather; then the piece is placed over the dome, allowing a lip at the top of the brim for attaching to crown. The wood brim mold is placed over the leather, which is on a flat surface. Weight the brim with books or bricks or clamp it to the surface.

The brim, trimmed and dried.

A hat need not conform exactly to the mold. Using the same mold *(above),* Bruce Vetter lifted the wet leather and pinched it into four folds. All leather will not do exactly what you want it to. This is the only piece of leather he was able to work into such perfect folds. Brim and crown were stitched together and the seam covered with a leather band and hardware.

WEED POTS. Joy Lobell. Pots, for a variety of uses,
may be sewn, stitched, or formed over a mold. They are
imaginatively shaped and executed by craftsmen and
accomplished artists.

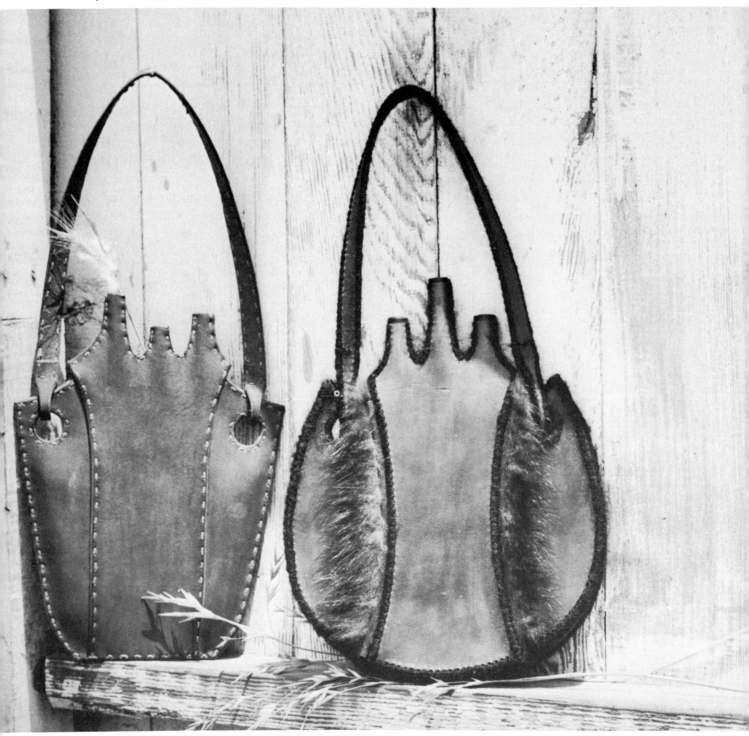

CHAPTER FIVE

Pots and Boxes

Individually styled pots and boxes are among the recent, unique applications of leather by creative craftsmen. These hanging or free-standing containers are often called "weed pots" because they are perfect for holding dried weeds and flowers. They might aptly be considered a functional art form. Pots and boxes are made by several methods: molding over a form, sewing soft leathers together, or laminating multiple layers of leather.

Pots often are combined with other media such as macramé (knotted cord) or carved wood handles in teak, cherry wood, ebony, and oak. Detailing may include some unusual applications of stamping, tooling, or hand stitching. Other details that have few counterparts in traditional Western leatherwork include wrapping with brass or natural fibers, tying in feathers and bones, gathering and puckering the leather, and combining finishes and colors on both the grain and flesh sides. African and Indian artifacts have inspired many unusual applications of detail.

Joy Lobell favors covering different-shaped boxes and combining her leather and suede constructions with fur, mirrors, and raised surface stitching. John Snidecor and John Cederquist exaggerate a seam and close the joint by working a lace of leather under the threads. The stitches joining seams may be those of embroidery, traditional lacing, and saddle stitching.

Murry Kusmin's laminated pots are constructed of multiple layers of leather carved with personal symbolic designs. Robert Henion has used molding techniques to create unique leather bottle forms. It is interesting to observe that none of the individual techniques used by these craftsmen is radically new; all involve tools and procedures described in Chapter 3.

On the accompanying pages in this chapter basic methods for making different three-dimensional pot and box forms are illustrated. Several details are emphasized to stimulate new combinations of materials and procedures. Use these examples as a jumping off point for your own pot and box forms. Combine some of the techniques mentioned in other parts of the book to make your boxes and pots—perhaps leathers that have been tie-dyed or batiked could be used successfully. Conversely, you can apply details shown for pots to other projects such as sculpture, macramé, or purses. The message is to mentally masticate the ideas and strive to evolve something that is uniquely yours.

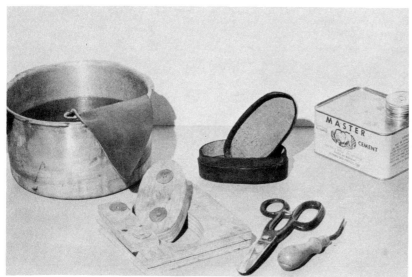

Bruce Vetter demonstrates one procedure for making formed leather shapes using a plywood mold, which really doesn't have to be a sophisticated device. Using a bandsaw, he cut a plug from a plywood square. The shaped plug is trimmed down about ¼ inch all around to allow for the thickness of leather to be placed in the socket. A brace of wood covers the cut made by the bandsaw. For deeper shapes, two layers of plywood are glued or bolted together. Edges that will accommodate leather are rounded and smoothed by sanding.

Two shapes taken from the illustrated mold are being stitched together. You can see where holes are punched for decorative wood pegs. This is the same process used for making gun cases, camera cases, and other formed shapes, but the artist has learned to "re-see" such shaping potential in new contexts.

Materials required to make a simple oval three-dimensional shape are minimal: a piece of 7- to 8-ounce vegetable-tanned shoulder or belly leather, the mold, warm water having a temperature under 180°F., cement, skive, and shears.

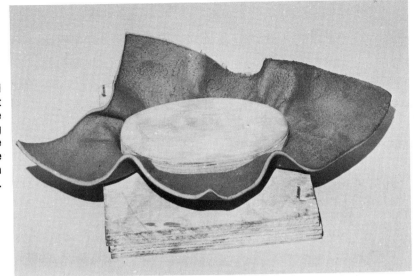

After the leather is saturated for five to ten minutes in hot water, it is placed over the hole of the wood mold and the plug forced in. Excess leather may be trimmed while wet or after the piece dries, using a French skive or a knife.

The leather should be smooth on the other side after it is forced into the mold. The usual recommendation is to allow the leather to dry in the mold for 24 hours. But Mr. Vetter has discovered that you can remove the plug after a few minutes and place the mold in a hot air furnace for about five minutes, or just long enough to dry the two outer surfaces and still have the leather retain its shape. He then removes the leather from the mold, colors it while wet, and sets it aside to dry overnight. Do not force dry leather by leaving it in an oven for a long time. This will bake the leather and make it brittle.

For a box and lid, two oval shapes are made. A third oval band is set in the bottom shape extending up about an inch. This extension will hold the lid. Glue the oval to the base, trim, dye, and finish edges.

HANGING POT. John Snidecor. Formed leather with hand carved
wood rim and handles. Wood pegs hold pot to neck. Oval punched
holes are laced through with a contrasting colored thread.
COURTESY, ARTIST

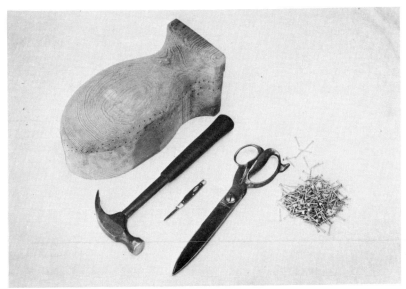

Making a pot form over a one-piece mold involves the same procedures as those shown for making a hat *(see Chapter 4).* John Snidecor carves a basic shape from soft pine.

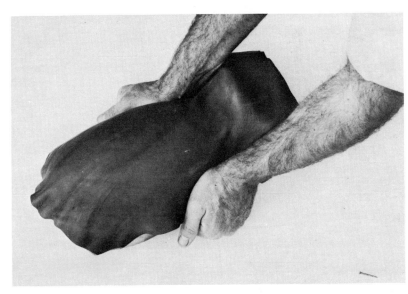

The leather is saturated and stretched over half the form (two of these will be made and combined). Four- to eight-ounce vegetable-tanned leather may be used for this procedure. While the leather is wet or after it is dry, a light-colored leather may be darkened by staining.

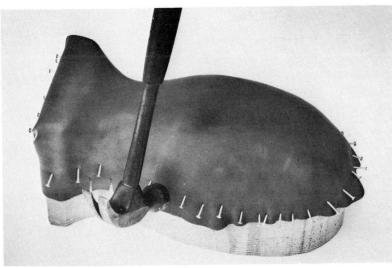

The leather is nailed with galvanized nails partially hammered into the mold at an angle. Dry the leather about 48 hours. The resulting shape is used to create the pot on page 82 or many variations, depending upon details, coloring, wood findings, and handles.

FORMED HANGING POT. Keith Klafs. 11 in. high,
7 in. wide without fringe. Seven-ounce cowhide
with a teakwood neck. Unusual wood pegging
is dome shaped. Saddle stitching at sides;
wrapping at bottom laces and around handle.

FORMED POT. Robert Henion. Wood findings
at sides of pot are designed to lace through rope
for macramé cords of twisted half knots.
(See Chapter 9, Macramé.)

WEED POT. Robert Henion. The leather for this exquisite pot
was stretched over a two-part wooden mold and allowed to dry.
The parts were then sewn together and the edges finished and dyed.
The neck was made from a separate piece of leather
and formed with a wooden dowel to make the opening.
Brass rings add textural contrast.

WEED POTS. Robert Henion. Pot shapes are made with two-part
wooden molds using the principles of stretching and forming.
For the necks of the pots the 7- to 8-ounce vegetable-tanned
leather was rewet, and a wood dowel 1 inch to 1½ inches
in diameter was inserted to make the opening. When dry, parts
of the pots are dyed, then punched and stitched with linen thread.
All pots are beautifully finished with oils and waxes. Macramé
cords and wood findings give added detail.

FORMED POT. Greg Tamminga. Lathe turned wood neck and wood buttons at seam. Brass wire wrapping over leather thong handle.

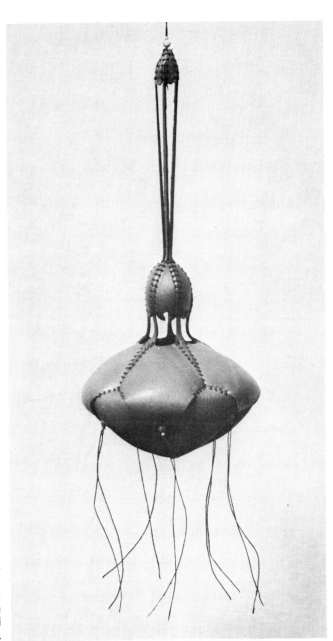

MODULAR HANGING POT. Larry Jones. Four-to six-ounce vegetable-tanned cowhide. Several pieces are carefully shaped over wood forms, then combined and stitched with black linen thread. Each stitched joint holds a strand of lace from the level below.

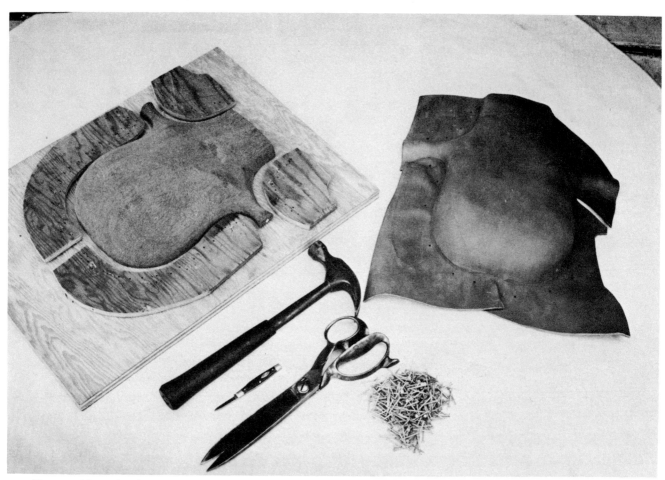

Forms with projections require innovative molds. The large shape
with projections is carved from mahogany and nailed or glued
to a sheet of plywood. Additional plywood shapes are fashioned
to conform to the outer line of the pot and to fit as jigsaw
puzzle parts.

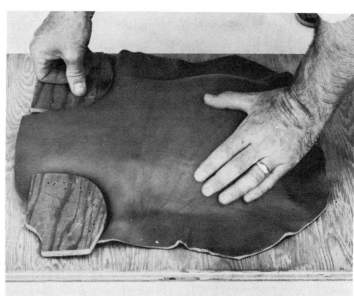

The wet leather is stretched over the mold;
then the pieces of plywood are fitted around the
basic shape. Use the tip end of the bone creaser
(page 45) to help crease the leather close to
the bottom of the mold.

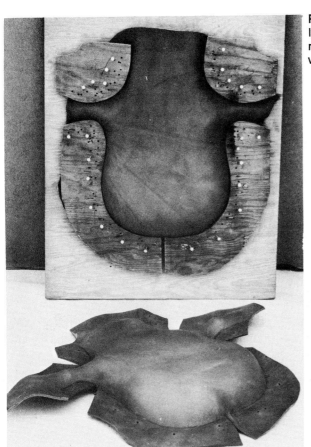

Plywood shapes are nailed in place to hold leather while drying for about 24 hours. Be sure nails are placed in outer rim of leather, which will be trimmed away.

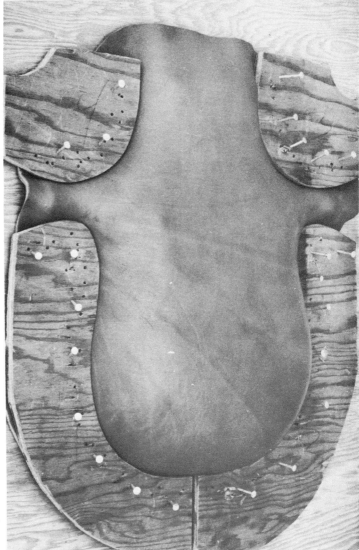

Two identical formed shapes will be stitched together to create the hanging container. The basic shape may be developed in scores of variations, depending upon the kind and shape of wood used at the neck, stitching, coloring, details, etc. Should you wish the neck or projecting shapes altered, rewet and insert a new form. Let the leather dry and remove the form.

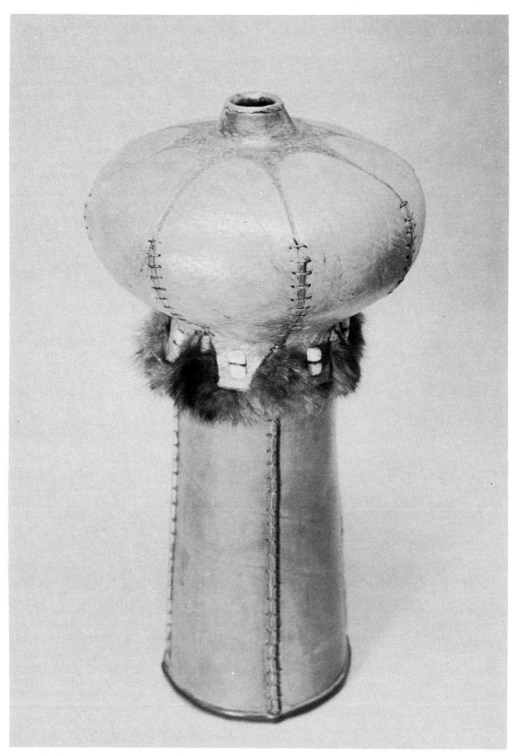

UNTITLED. John Cederquist. 13 in. high, 8 in. top diameter. Leather has been cut and stitched to achieve the dome top, but a dowel is placed in the neck hole to stretch and mold the leather. The base is shaped and stitched, and pieces are combined with ivory and mink. Some tooling and carving are used. Basically, this is a container, but it has all the attributes of sculpture.

DETAILS OF POT *(left)*

The tooling around the top of this piece is a contemporary example of the use of the stippling stamp. The tooling is a darker brown than the body of the work.

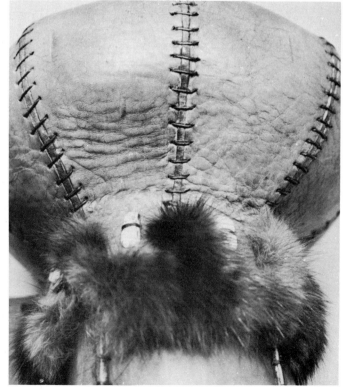

Black linen stitching holds the split forms of the crown, and the seam itself is filled in with a strip of matching leather lacing placed evenly with the surface of the leather. Seams on the base of the pot are pieces of narrow stripped leather placed on top of the surface and stitched to it for an added relief design. The extra rim at the base finishes the bottom edge. *(See photo page 88.)*

HANGING POT. Joy Lobell. Suede with leather and fur.

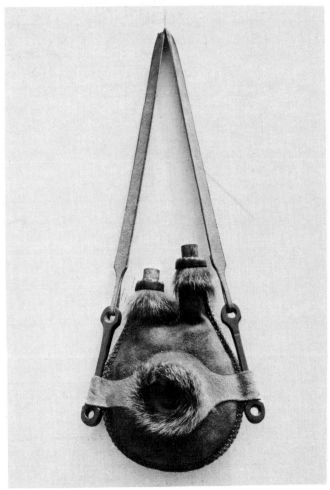

DOUBLE SPOUT POT. Joy Lobell. Suede with fur and wood findings. Decorative thread-stitched edges.

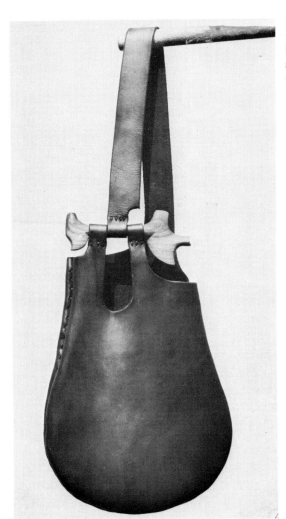

LATIGO POUCH. John Cederquist. Soft leather pouch simply and elegantly designed with a hand carved, pegged wood handle. One inside seam at bottom and one outside seam at side contribute to the pouch's asymmetry.

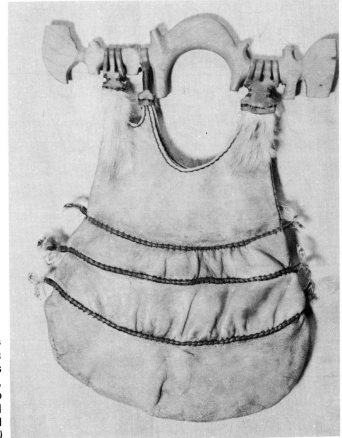

POUCH. John Cederquist. 15 in. high. Shapes of leather are stitched together using a complementary colored piece of thong across the stitched seam. Ends of thongs are wrapped, and a chicken feather is added. Wrapping also holds the leather to the hand carved cherry wood handle. Fur details added. Bottom seam is blind stitched from the inside. *(See page 42 for detail.)*

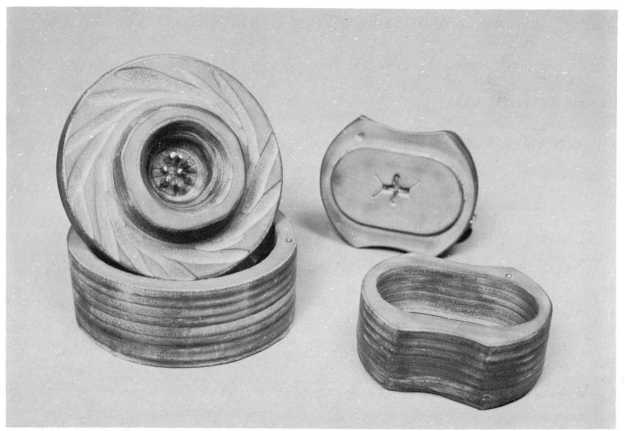

LAMINATED POTS. Murry Kusmin. Shapes of pots can vary; edges may be
smooth or overlapping. Note "key" nail in base and indentation in lid
so cover fits correctly as noted in step six of the demonstration
(bottom photo page 81). Volcanic-shaped lid of pot at left results from
building up several smaller circles on top of the lid. Additional laminated
pots are shown on page 68.

POTENTIAL OF LAMINATING LEATHER

Sizes and shapes of pieces available in
leather are only as thick or wide as an original hide. To achieve shapes thicker or
larger than the original requires laminating or gluing one or more layers of leather
together. The ability to laminate can
suggest unexplored potential for creative
leatherwork.

Laminate 8 to 14 ounces of the same
sizes or assorted thicknesses and colors of
leathers; then carve the shape you want
out of the piece as though it were a solid
block. You can edge-glue thick layers for
slab constructions, using the same principles as the woodworker who builds boxes
and tables. When laminating, you can project portions of layers from the main piece
or create forms that will jut precariously
into space with or without an armature.
You can construct odd, short, and tall
boxes, such as those Murry Kusmin has
made from sole leather.

Surfaces to be laminated should be
roughened up before applying the contact
cement for adhering. When cements are
dry, laminated leather may be carved,
shaped with hand woodworking or power
tools, sanded, colored, and finished as in
any other leather procedure.

Materials for making laminated pots include two circular cutters, a scraper, skiver, contact cement, 12-ounce cowhide, wood carving tools, edge beveler, and awl. Other items not shown are an electric drill for smoothing, beeswax, finishing oils, and polishing waxes.

Two circular arch dies are used to cut the circles: the larger has a 3-inch diameter; the smaller for the inside negative has a 2-inch diameter. (Save these negatives for other uses.) Solid 3-inch circles are also needed: three for the lid and one for the base.

Also a 2-inch solid circle is needed for the base of the cover to fit inside the diameter of pot. Observe that the circles are cut a few inches apart rather than right next to each other. The leftover areas will become bracelet strips.

Scrape the surfaces of the leather so the contact cement will make a thorough adhesion. Sand and finish the inside wall of the laminated rings before cementing to the base circle. Carve any details desired on the upper surface of the base circle before adhering.

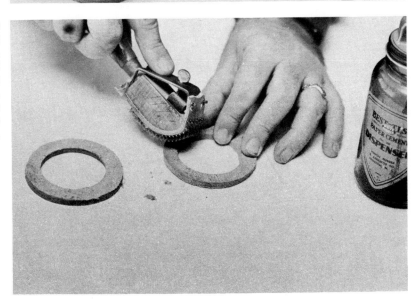

For Murry, the lid is the most fun. He cuts off-center within the circle so that one layer is exposed differently under another; then he begins carving with any tool that will do the job regardless of the stated function of the tool.

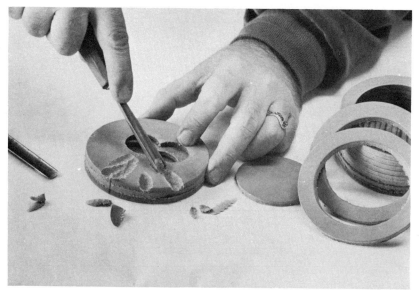

Murry uses the skive as an edge carving tool and, as with any improvised approach, continues to develop his design. Here he simulates caves. At the bottom of the lid, a 2-inch diameter circle—the size of the inside diameter of the pot—is glued to make a tight-fitting cover. A brass nail is placed at the rim of the cover and keyed to an indentation in the pot rim for a consistent cover placement.

Edges are water moistened and, while wet, smoothed and polished with the sanding drum of an electric drill that has been dipped in beeswax. The final step will be for Murry to tuck two round-headed brass nails deep within the caves to represent refugees in his series of "refugee pots."

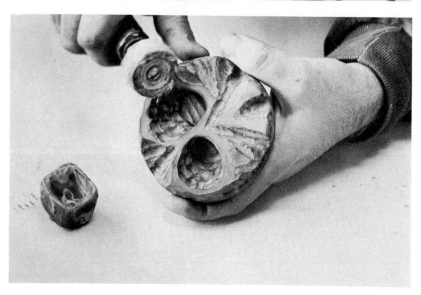

REFUGEE POT. Murry Kusmin. The finished pot has been lightly stained, waxed, and buffed.

CRATER POT. Murry Kusmin. The crater effect is achieved by gouging a series of graduated shapes from three laminated circles.

BOX. Murry Kusmin. For a square or rectangular box, strips of 12-ounce cowhide are laminated one on top of another for the base; for the lid, half circles on each side determine the curve. The lid is one piece of leather carved to appear as strips and to coordinate with the base of the box. The contrasting bands on each end of the lid are functional as well as decorative because they hide butted leather edges. The box is hinged at the back.

CONSTRUCTION. Megan Lloyd Hill. 30 in. high, 20 in. wide. Bluish white
suede is laminated to a framed wood construction; the skull
and oval backing are attached with crews or bolts. PHOTO, KARL KERNBERGER

CHAPTER SIX

Collages and Constructions

Using leather for art forms such as collages and constructions is only beginning to be done by artists. The works illustrated in this chapter have been selected because they show varieties of leathers and techniques for expressive artistic statements.

To make a collage, you need only a wood, Masonite, or canvas backing, scissors, glue, and pieces of used or new leather. Formal techniques for leatherworking may be ignored and the leather used much as a paper or fabric collage medium. You may prefer roughly textured edges to those that are finely burnished as they are on a belt or sandal. Stitching may be nonexistent, haphazard, or elaborate. Skiving may be required to accomplish a specific effect. The main ingredient is imagination. The final judgment is based on good design and ultimately on "doing what works."

In addition to combining techniques in collages and constructions, artists combine leather with found objects such as chains, clock parts, fabrics, bones, skeletons, rope, and fur. Among the novel and successful uses of leather and mixed media are the collages by Ruben Steinberg. He likes leather because of its textures and densities, often coloring it with thinned-down paints, sometimes burning it with a torch for a curled effect, and even using it to make shapes for printmaking.

Megan Lloyd Hill strives for and succeeds to impart a unity, silence, beauty, and sense of the unknown in her wood constructions covered with colorful suedes and garment leathers. These are background for stark dried bones from the New Mexico desert, leather, shells, and other found objects.

Mike Selig stretches leather over hoops and squares, often using it in torn and tattered shapes for a statement that combines natural wood, bone shapes, and feathers in a beautiful, organically integrated work that reflects his personal attachment to nature. Caroline Montague's use of leather in flat collage, deep relief, and sculpture is possible because of the nature of leather and the underlying framework made from wood or welded metal.

In approaching collage making use the accompanying examples to stimulate ideas; then start out on your own. Use leather as a medium of expression in personal ways, in any direction your whims take you. Push the leather around a bit, use it wet or dry, stretch it, cut it, crumple it, pleat it. Remember, there are no rules for this kind of work. Just save all your leather scraps and other types of odds and ends; then get them all together and start developing collages and constructions until you have something you are pleased with.

COLLAGE. Caroline Montague.
PHOTO, COURTESY ARTIST

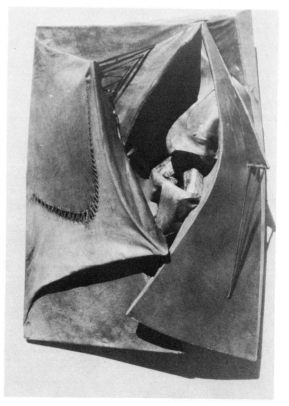

RELIEF COLLAGE. Caroline Montague.
PHOTO, COURTESY ARTIST

CONSTRUCTION. Caroline Montague.
PHOTO, COURTESY ARTIST

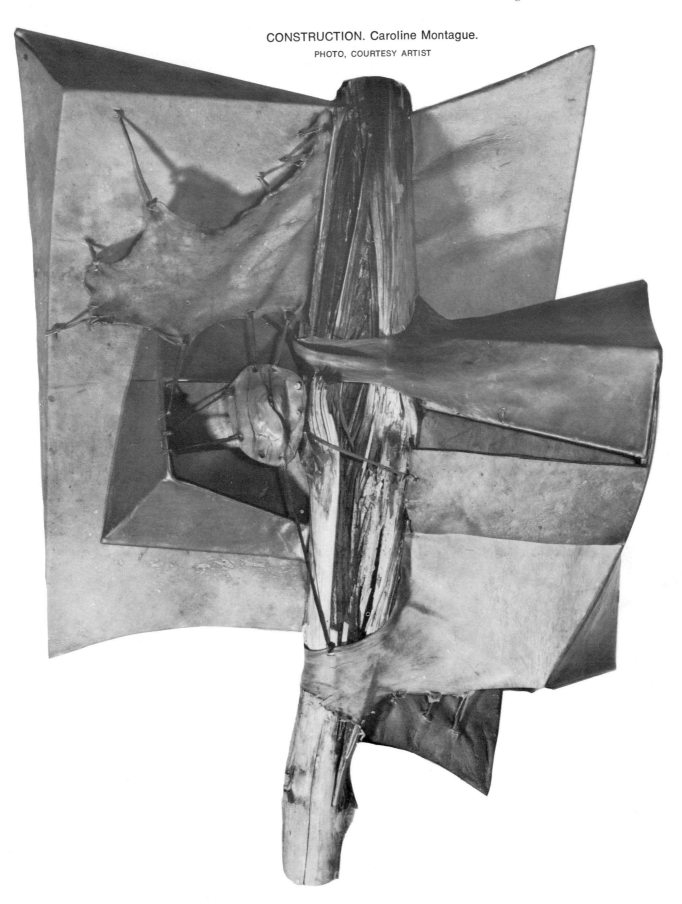

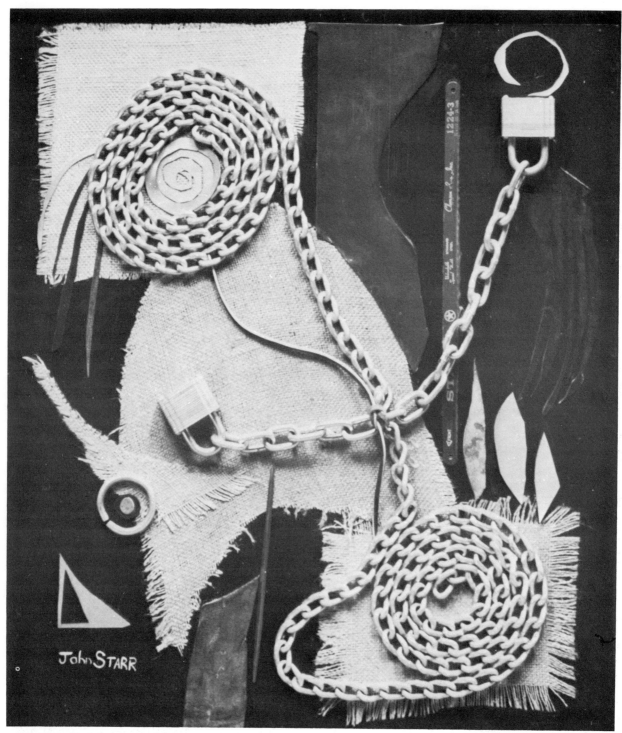

BONDAGE. John Starr. Collage with leather,
chains, burlap, and miscellaneous found objects.

UNTITLED. Ruben Steinberg, Leather, rope, textiles, and found objects all are carefully controlled in their relationships and combinations.

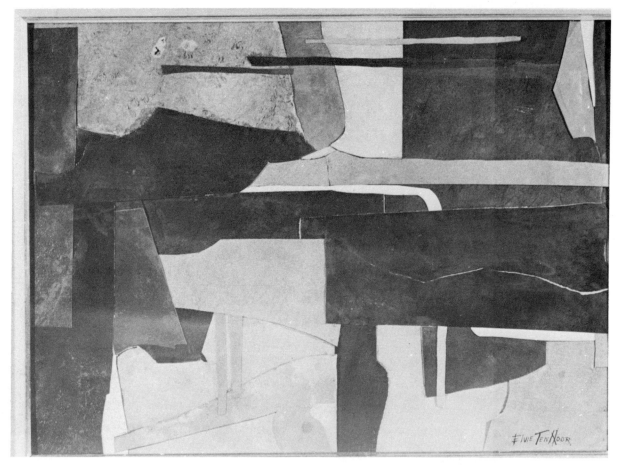

THE OLD PIANO. Elvie Ten Hoor. Both sides of cut shapes of suede and leather are used for different textures in this collage.

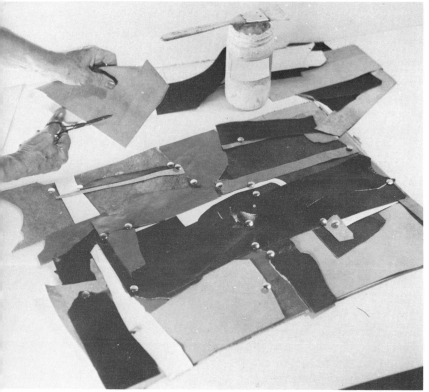

The composition is planned by tacking shapes into place on a masonite backing, then gluing them. Household glues or rubber cement easily can be used for leather collage pieces. These glues give you the option of picking up the pieces and moving them around if you are not satisfied with a first placement.

NOVEMBER LANDSCAPE.
Mike Selig. 32 in. diameter.
Leather, rawhide, fur, feathers,
wool, polyester resin, and
chrome.

COLLECTION: MISS JUDITH EHRICH,
SANTA FE, N.M.

FAWN SONG. Mike
Selig. 32 in. diameter.
Leather, fur, feathers,
fabric, deer skull with
antlers, and paint.

MATADOR. John Starr. Scrap
leather in black, red,
white, and yellow.

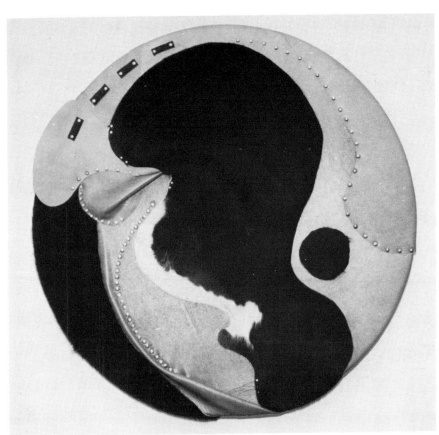

PONDEROSA FLIGHT. Elisabet
Siewert-Miller. 40 in. diameter.
Fur assemblage on round plaque
combining leather, metal
buttons, and rivets.
PHOTO, CANNON

COMPUTER NIGHTMARE.
Ruben Steinberg. Laminated
leathers combined with ropes,
computer parts, and gears.

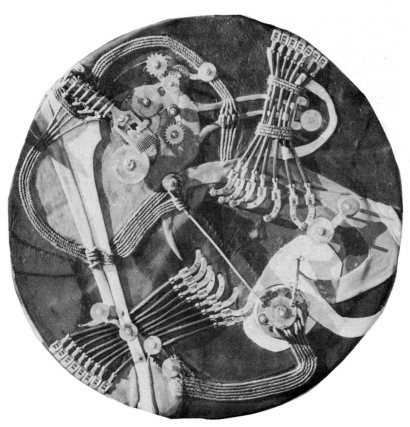

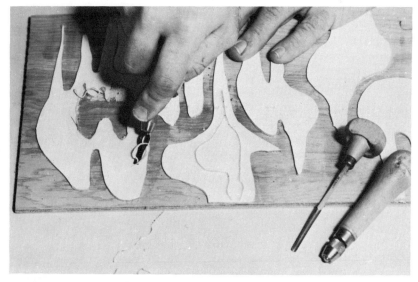

Ruben Steinberg here shares some of his unusual methods for working with leather that can yield unusual effects in a collage. Often, by using techniques applied to other media, he creates surprising combinations. At left, he began by using shapes of 3-ounce white kid glued to a board. He cut the shapes out and dug grooves in them with a linoleum cutter, intending to use the board for pulling prints on paper.

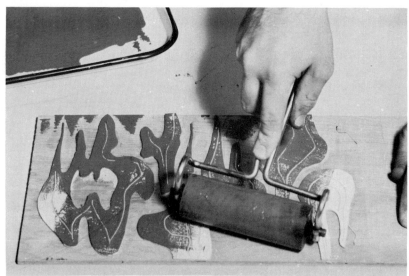

He then inked the shapes with a brayer and water-base printer's ink as you would ink a wood or linoleum block . . .

. . . and pulled a print.

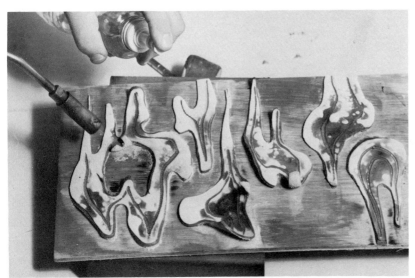

Then Ruben Steinberg decided to see what would happen if he used a propane torch on the leather. Applying the flame with one hand, he kept a spray bottle of water in the other to douse any burning. The leather, colored from the printing ink, began to curl and twist; the surface was charred. Intrigued, he put the board aside for further work and experimentation.

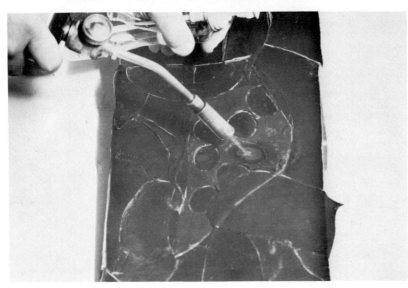

Applying the heat from a propane torch to glued scraps of leftover leather from policemen's uniforms, Mr. Steinberg burned holes through from one layer to another for interesting shapes and textures, always keeping the spray bottle of water ready in the other hand to put out any excess burning.

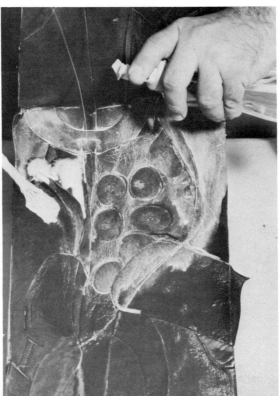

To bring out the texture of the piece, he applied dabs of acrylic paint to the surface and sprayed it with water so the paint would thin and run into the cracks and edges of the leather.

CITYSCAPE. Ruben Steinberg. Scraps of a variety of leather in both flat planes and dimensional relief are painted with artists' acrylics and combined with glued rope in knotted, twisted, and wound directions resulting in a highly tactile quality.

Detail of above.

ILLUSIONS OF WATER. Murry Kusmin. Scraps and negatives from cutting soles, barrettes, circles, etc. are cemented and nailed to a wooden background for this relief composition in warm brown dyed shoulder cowhide.

Detail of above. Snake-like shapes and negatives are formed within an area by wetting and shaping the leather much in the same way as you would work with shapes of clay. Edges may be beveled and skived to reflect light differently.

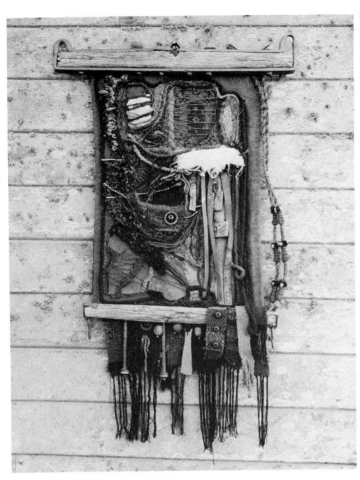

HANGING. Barbara Waszak Chapman. Leather, ceramics, beading, old hardware, and other materials on wood.

COURTESY: PASADENA ART MUSEUM, PASADENA, CALIF. PHOTO, RICHARD GROSS

CONSTRUCTION. Megan Lloyd Hill. 28 in. high, 23 in. wide. Beige and white suede with aluminum, feathers, and beads of bone.

PHOTO, KARL KERNBERGER

THE BEAST, IF NOT THE FRAME,
CONTAINED. Murry Kusmin.
24 in. square. Cut and shaped
cowhide is laminated and nailed
to a wood backing with pieces
of jaguar fur pulled in and out
of the leather. The frame is
partially leather.

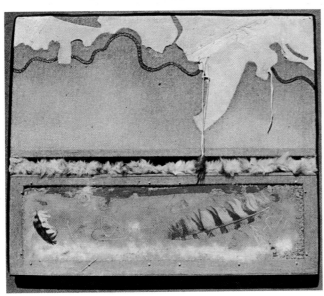

UNTITLED. Mike Selig. 25 in. wide,
22 in. high. A rectangular collage of
leather, fabric, paint, fur,
earth, and mixed fragments
such as pot shard, metal,
feathers, string, etc.

SCULPTURE. Caroline Montague. Stretched leather over
a metal armature. COURTESY, ARTIST

CHAPTER SEVEN

Sculpture

It is not difficult to think of functional three-dimensional leather objects: gun or camera cases, purses, lamps—the list is endless. When craft magazines print articles on leather art, they usually discuss surface tooling and decorating and not the form itself.

Therefore, the idea of leather sculpture must be considered an event, a newcomer along with lights, plastics, and metals in the current realm of art materials. All of these materials have been in existence for years, of course, but in other contexts. Now, the artist has reached into the industrial pile and pulled out some different materials with which to work.

The sculptor usually has served a long apprenticeship and has complete knowledge of design and form. In his never ending search for avenues of expression, he discovers the potential of leather. Leather wet. Leather dry. Leather that can be molded as clay and stretched as a completely tensile fabric. Leather that can be hammered, drilled, laminated, scored, carved, sewn, made soft or hard. Leather has all these varieties, plus being suitable for coloring. With experimentation, trial and error, the sculptor evolves a way that pleases him. So he creates.

To overcome problems of size and to build a three-dimensional form, the sculptor can laminate to achieve large pieces that can be carved or worked in myriad ways. He can build an armature, or framework, over which the leather can be pulled and positioned. He can leave open space within the form so that negative areas become part of the composition; or he can close up space, using complementary interlocking shapes. The sculptor can give his work a rough-textured finish or a highly polished one.

In addition to leather as a major part of your composition, don't hesitate to bring other media into play. Caroline Montague allows her welded-iron or carved-wood armatures to show as a textured contrast to the leather. Nancy Grossman employs many of the findings and techniques used by the shoemaker, dressmaker, and leather-worker in her carved wood heads covered with leather. Fred Borcherdt likes the "volume" of closed rather than open pieces. Jack Kearney's sculptures are composed of stripped, hanging pieces of leather attached to handshaped wood and wire frames. Kearney also includes found objects, carved ivory pieces, and welded metal parts.

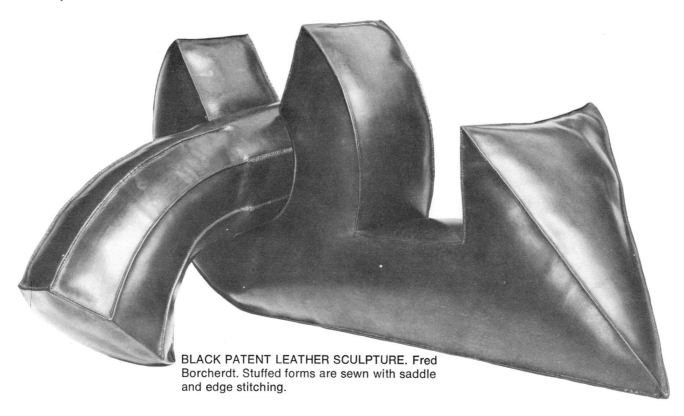

BLACK PATENT LEATHER SCULPTURE. Fred
Borcherdt. Stuffed forms are sewn with saddle
and edge stitching.

DANCERS WITH CHILD. Murry Kusmin. Laminated pieces
of cowhide over brass rods are set into a frame. Pieces
rotate freely for changing spatial relationships.

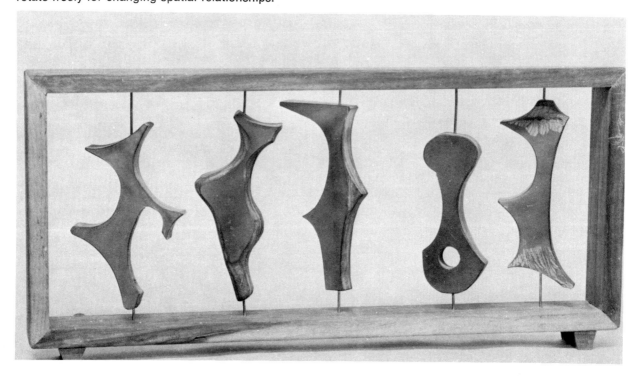

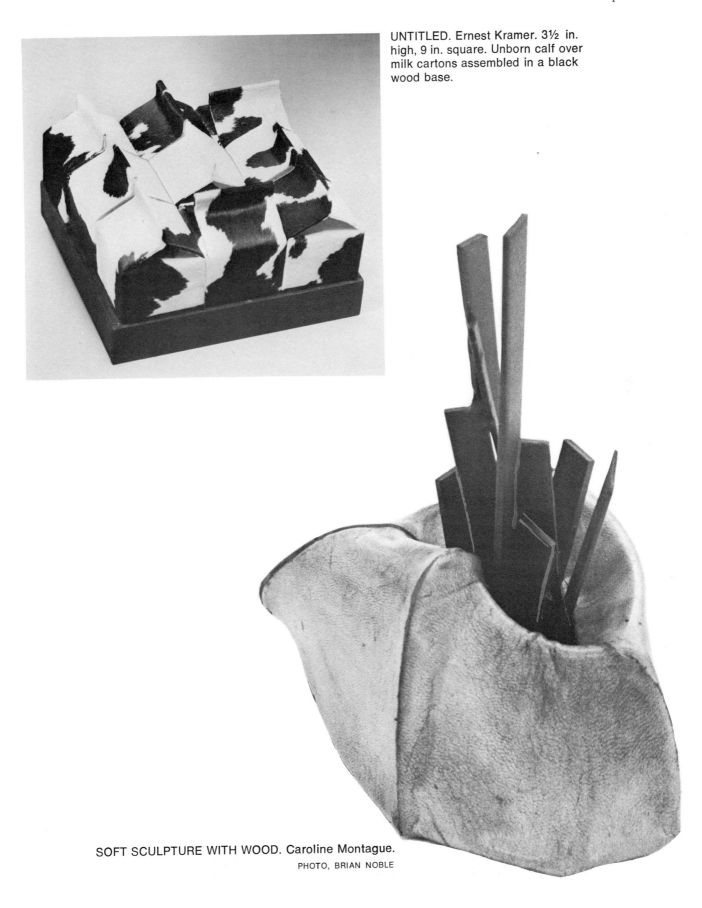

UNTITLED. Ernest Kramer. 3½ in. high, 9 in. square. Unborn calf over milk cartons assembled in a black wood base.

SOFT SCULPTURE WITH WOOD. Caroline Montague.

PHOTO, BRIAN NOBLE

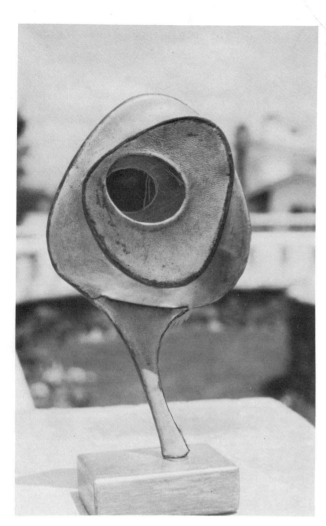

SCULPTURE. Caroline Montague.
4 ft. high. Stretched leather over a
frame with painting.

Rear view of above.

BST. Nancy Grossman. 16 in.
high. Leather over carved
wood head.

COURTESY, CORDIER & EKSTROM, INC.,
NEW YORK

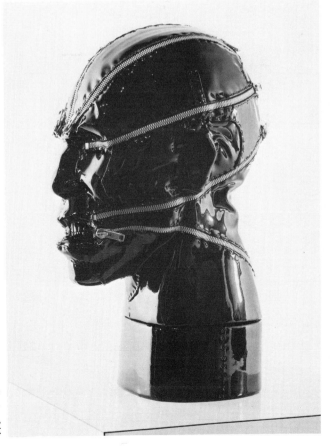

T.Y.V.L. Nancy Grossman. 15 in.
high. Patent leather over carved wood.

COURTESY, CORDIER & EKSTROM, INC.,
NEW YORK

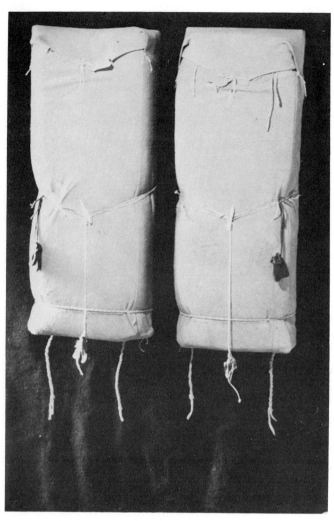

TWO BAGS. Mike Selig. Stuffed leather, sewn and wrapped. Bone and deer hooves added.

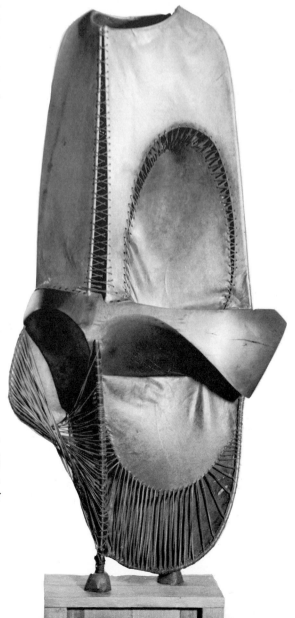

CONSTRUCTION NO. 29. Caroline Montague. 6 ft. high. Leather stretched, laced, and formed over a metal frame.

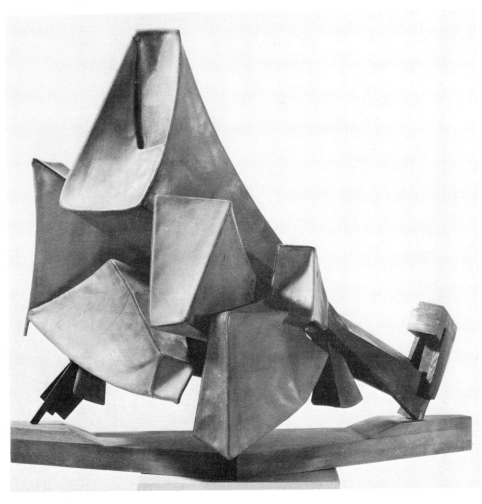

CONSTRUCTION NO. 31.
Caroline Montague.
Goatskin stretched and
stitched over wood
and iron frame.

COURTESY,
NORTH CAROLINA MUSEUM OF ART

THESE CHAINS, MINE,
YOURS. Murry Kusmin.
Laminated ovals. Inter-
linked and movable
laminated ovals are
mounted at one point
on a wood base.

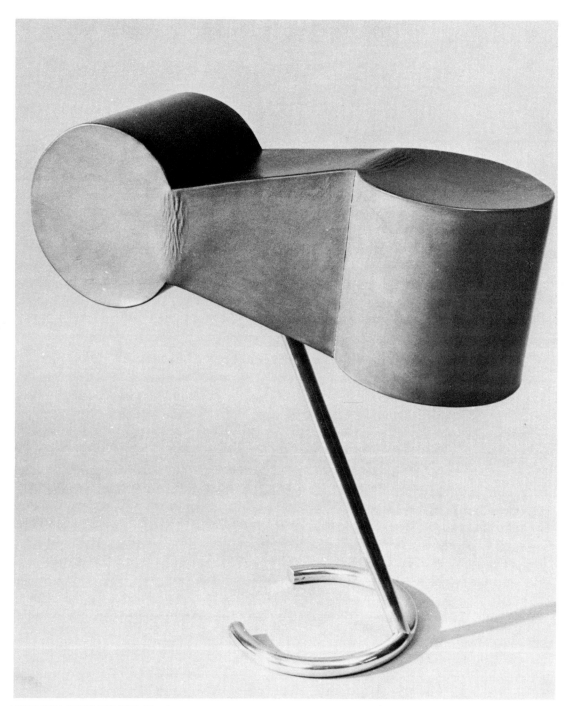

FORMED SCULPTURE. Fred
Borcherdt. 20 in. high. Leather
mounted on welded brass base.

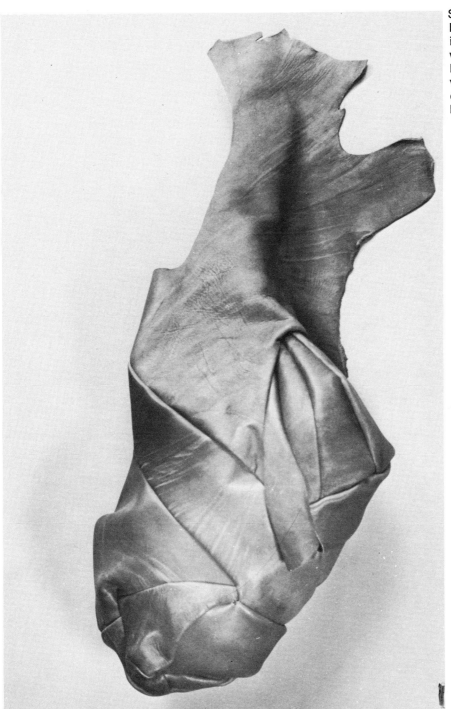

SOFT SCULPTURE. Ernest Kramer. 37 in. high, 17 in. wide, 9½ in. deep. Four- to five-ounce vegetable-tanned cowhide. Parts are hand dyed.

HIPPIE IN A PHONE BOOTH. Jack Kearney. Life-size
figure made over a wood and chicken wire frame, then
covered with layers of stripped colored leather. Hand
and face are carved of wood, and the figure is placed
in an outdated telephone booth.

TWO-HEADED TOUCAN. Jack Kearney. The leather wrapping is scalloped and stripped to make this fantasy feathered friend with carved ivory bills and welded metal legs.

CRANE. Jack Kearney. 4 ft. high. Shapes of colored leather (both grain and flesh side in a variety of grains and colors) from a shoe findings supplier are used to simulate the bird's natural coloring. Layers of leather are laid over a carved wood body, which has an ivory bill and welded iron legs.

ROOSTER. Jack Kearney. On all these pieces, leather is nailed, stapled, and cemented in place.

MOTHER IN HER NEW EASTER
BONNET. Murry Kusmin. With his
whimsical sense of humor and the
addition of carving and coloring,
Murry created this appealing
sculpture utilizing scraps of
sole leather.

THE ASSAULT. Murry Kusmin. By
bending, combining, carving,
staining, and polishing leftover
pieces of sole leather, you can
create an endless number of
sculptural forms that suggest
myriad ideas. For extra thickness,
pieces may be laminated; they may
have metal rods introduced for
support and additional design
qualities and may be mounted on a
wood or leather base.

CHAPTER EIGHT

Using Scrap Imaginatively

Getting the optimum finished items from a piece of leather and minimizing the amount of waste requires careful planning. It is in planning uses for scrap that the experienced craftsman who makes a living from leatherwork can show the part-time craftsman a few tricks. At Murry Kusmin's leather shop in Hyannis, Massachusetts, the cutting of various hides is carefully planned before any cutting is actually done. Murry doesn't waste an ounce of leather if he can help it.

For example, a beginner who wants a series of circles or ovals might cut them so close to one another that he has no usable leftover scraps. However, if the circles are placed a short distance apart, the negative areas can be used to make a variety of items such as keyrings, earrings, jewelry parts, rings, sculptures, and collages. The same is true when cutting soles for shoes or sandals; many of the negative areas from a sheet from which soles have been cut find a new life in sculpture, as part of a room-dividing screen (see Chapter 14), or as a lamp shade. Often, if the negative space is carefully planned, the piece has an interesting enough shape in itself to be a wall hanging or construction.

The idea is to get the most mileage from a piece of leather, whether leatherworking is your business or hobby. Even the blanks left from the oval, oblong, and round punches should be saved in a jar; they can become eyes for animals, strung as beads for room dividers, strung at the end of a macramé cord, or glued to any flat surface to create a two-dimensional appearance.

The leftover blank of a sole leather negative cut into a circle makes an attractive design by itself. The sole cuts were planned with the leftover design in mind. The piece might be mounted flat on a board or with a peg under the center to give a dimensional quality to the piece. The potential of scraps should delight anyone with a little imagination.

123

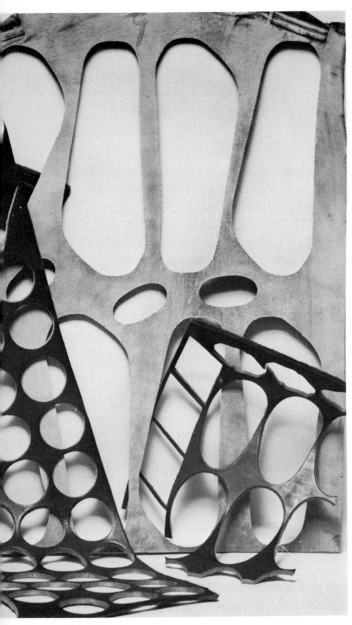

When cutting into leathers, plan to leave leftovers that can become additional objects. By cutting circles far enough apart, the leftover areas may be used for earring shapes, keychains, unusual shaped bracelets, pendants, mobile and collage parts. Cutting the circles closer together probably would result not in any more circles but only in greater waste areas. Learn to visualize leftover shapes as objects rather than simply leftovers.

Earrings made from scraps prevent costly waste: an important factor for the craftsman who goes into business. Notice that the end of the earring where the finding is inserted is skived. This permits it to lie flat next to the earlobe. The two pairs of rectangular earrings are unusual; the pair at the rear of the photo has a central rectangle pegged at top and bottom, so it is movable. This pair is made of two layers of cowhide with the nail inserted between the layers. The bottom pair utilizes punched dots that are colored a contrasting shade and reinserted into the earring for added detail.

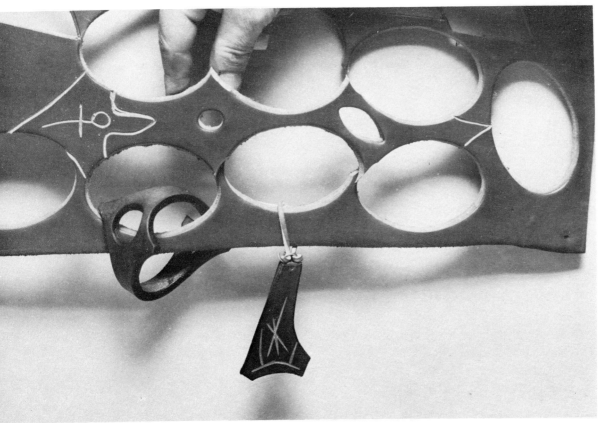

Murry Kusmin illustrates how a bracelet with an unusual shape is planned from the leftover leather between ovals. The round and oval holes that were punched for earrings become part of the negative pattern of the bracelet. The bottom piece is used for a keychain. The two pieces are laminated, lightly carved, and colored. Carving with a linoleum cutting tool to dig below the surface exposes the natural color of the leather. Edges should be colored and burnished.

BRACELETS. Murry Kusmin. A variety of inventive areas of scrap, including twisted industrial belting (left), is used for bracelets. Blanks from holes are used for earrings.

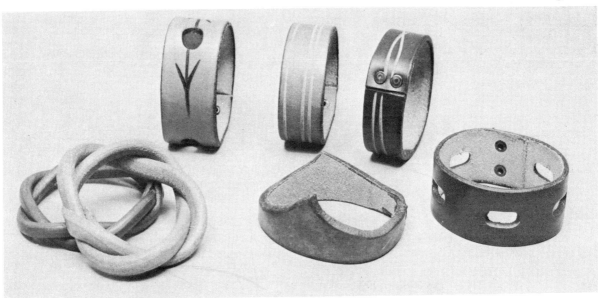

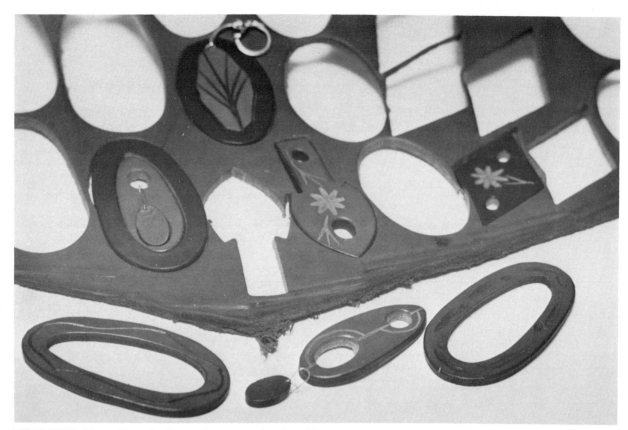

KEY RINGS. Murry Kusmin. In another example of making the most of a
piece of hide, ovals, arrows, and rectangles have been cut for key rings and
barrettes. Inner punchings become shapes for earrings.

BARRETTES. Murry
Kusmin. A series of
barrettes are made from
various shapes of cow-
hide and industrial
leather belting, which is
available in various
diameters from industrial
supply firms. You also
can buy some belting
in hardware stores.
Crossover barrettes are
cemented and tacked in
the center. The carving
is done with a wood
cutting tool. Edges of
flat leather pieces are
beveled and burnished.

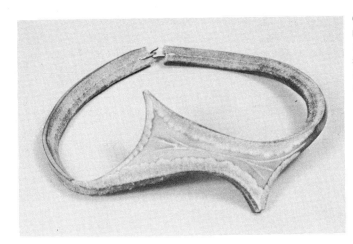

CHOKER. Murry Kusmin. By now, you should be able to recognize that the entire shape was utilized from between sole cuttings, then carved and stained.

NECKLACE AND EARRING SET. Murry Kusmin. "Chain" of industrial leather belting; "jewels" are scrap pieces of 10- to 12-ounce cowhide.

BRACELETS AND RINGS. Murry Kusmin. Accessories such as these can be the backbone of the leather crafter's stock and usually are made from carefully planned cuttings.

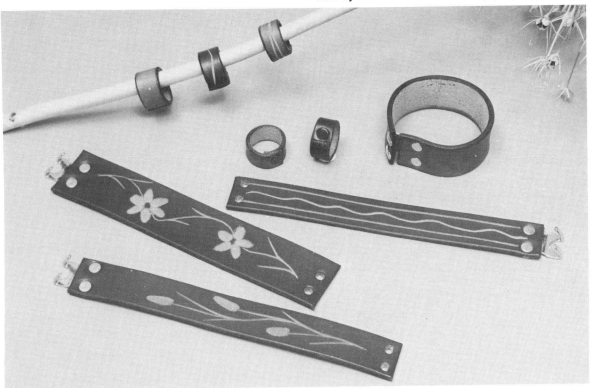

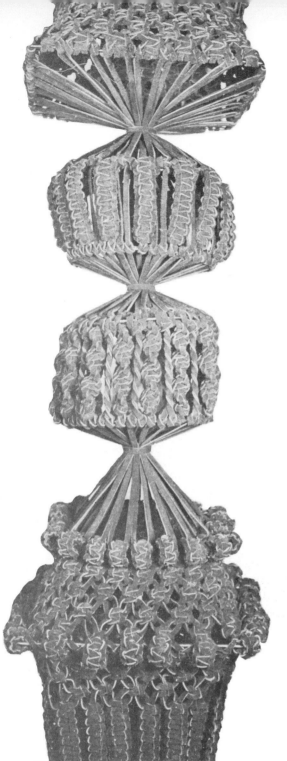

LEATHER HANGING. Lynn Doran. One large hide was stripped to leave solid portions for the top, which was stitched in panels. Some strips were added in the center and combined with beige linen cords for the interior circumference of knots. Clove hitches are used for horizontal knotting; loose and tight square knots are tied for verticals.

SPACE HANGING. Gloria Crouse. Stripped beige cowhide is tied over metal rectangles and circles to create a three-dimensional hanging. Tied with square knots and half knot twists, the connected total piece has an unusual sculptural volume.

CHAPTER NINE

Macramé

Macramé is the recently revived ancient technique of tying knots to make jewelry, vests, dresses, hangings, and sculpture. Once practiced prodigiously by sailors to while away long shipboard hours, today macramé is considered to be a textile art.

With only two basic knots, the clove hitch and square knot, you can make unlimited designs. You can use leather thongs and laces for knotting, and leather as an adjunct to knotting with fiber cords. The only problem in using leather is that animal hides are limited in length, so you must be inventive to achieve long cords required for ambitious projects.

Leather can be lengthened by skiving and cementing ends. Lengths also may be stripped from circles. You may use round and flat leather or latigo and vinyl lacing, which comes in 25- to 100-yard spools. The simplest procedure, of course, is to plan short projects so you can use short laces and lengths of stripped hide.

To start knotting, fold several cords in half and mount them with a lark's head knot across a holding line made of another cord, a piece of punched leather, a dowel, or any type of rod or twig. The only other items required are U-shaped pins (from any do-it-yourself upholstery counter), a

square of polyurethane or other foam cushioning that will accept the pins, and a cutting knife or scissors. Some people prefer to knot without a backing and devise holders such as a curtain rod or the back of a chair.

It is difficult to estimate lengths of cord necessary for knotting in any particular material; it depends on the thickness of the cord and how tightly you tie the knots. A rough estimate is to use a cord four times as long as the desired length of the finished piece. However, to give you a better idea of how much cord you will need, it's good practice to make a knotting sample before you begin a whole project. Take a given length of cord, knot it, then determine how much cord you used to make the knot. Also measure the number of cords required to make one inch horizontally, and then multiply the number of knots per inch by the desired width in inches.

When knotting, be as inventive as possible with variations of knot patterns, progressions, and number of cords used for a knot. Knots may be tied close together or far apart; beads and objects may be added.

Rawhide lacing is used in the knotting illustrations in this chapter. The advantage of rawhide and vegetable-tanned cowhide strips over other types of lacing is that by wetting them you can smooth and stretch the piece. After knotting, wetting the finished macramé will result in knots that hold tightly. Also by wetting the leather the piece may be shaped to fit the body or to conform to a curve or sculptural dimension.

When integrating solid pieces of leather with fiber cords, use your revolving punch, stitching marker, groover, and thonging chisels to make holes and slits for mounting the cords. The lark's head knot is frequently used alone for adding fringing to vests, pants, and ponchos. Additional knotting on fringes adds more interest.

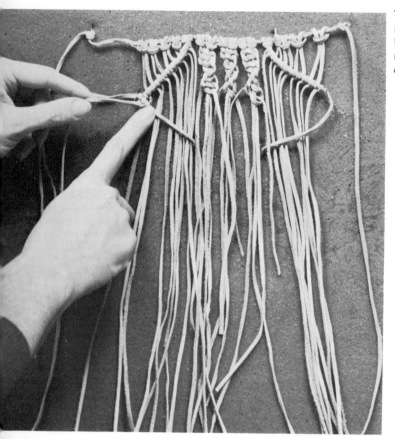

The basic set-up for macramé includes a foam backing that will accept "U" pins, a holding line, and the knotting cords. The holding line may be a length of leather, a branch, wood dowel rod, metal bar, etc.

For three-dimensional forms, the knotted cords may be suspended from leather with holes punched to accept cords of other materials as well as leather strips. Detail from a hanging by John Faulkner.

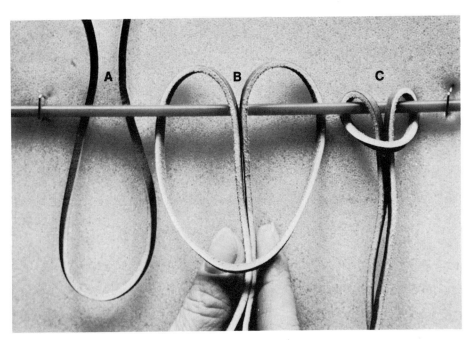

The lark's head is the best way to mount cords for macramé.

A. Bend the cord in half and from the top slide it under the holding line that is pinned to board.

B. Pull the loose ends over the holding line and under the loop.

C. Pull the loose ends through and you have the finished lark's head, which gives you two strands for knotting.

A row of cords mounted to the edge of a rope with the lark's head may remain with only the mounting knot, or additional knots may be tied to form an attractive border. Because of the textures of suede and leather, knots hold beautifully and do not slip as they might in other knotting materials.

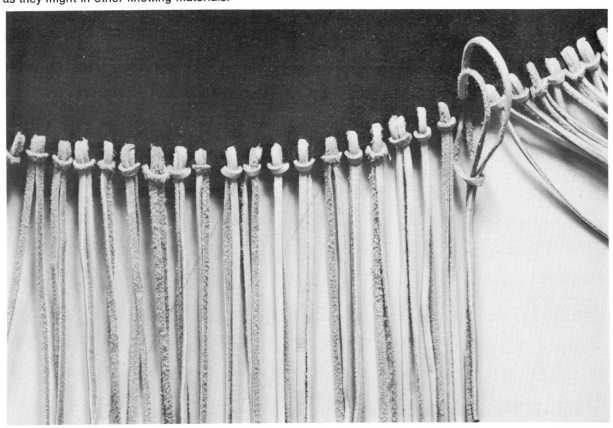

SQUARE KNOT

Each square knot requires four strands (two cords folded in half and mounted). Mount six cords on a line so you have twelve strands, a good beginning for practice. In the accompanying illustrations 54-inch rawhide shoe laces are used. For longer knotting, these laces are available in 108 inches and may be skived and ce-mented for even longer laces. You can practice with any cord, string, or yarn.

Consider the two central cords, anchor cords and the two outside cords, knotting cords. The procedure is to tie the knotting cords over the anchor cords. The following instructions correspond with the photos.

A. Bring the right knotting cord over to the left of the two anchor cords.

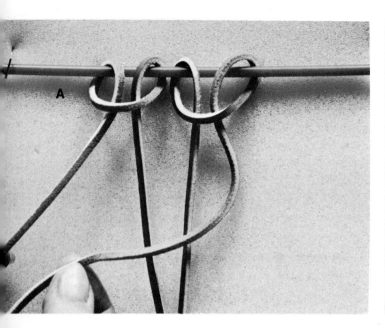

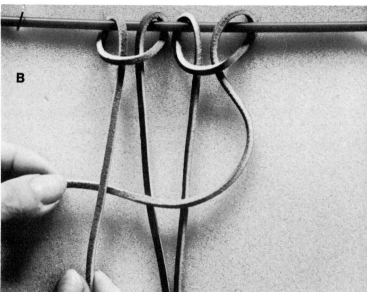

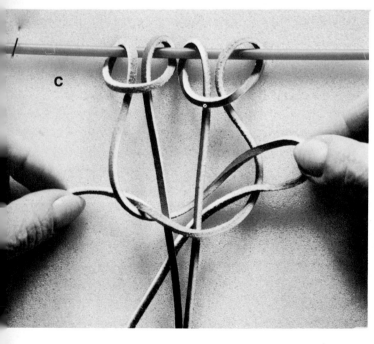

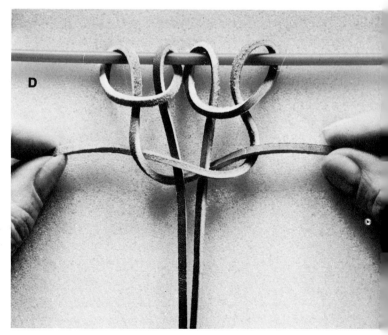

B. Place the left knotting cord over the right.

C. Bring the left cord under the anchors and up through the loop formed by the right cord.

D. Pull, and you have the first half of the square knot.

For the second half of the knot, follow the same procedure as the preceding but now knot to the *right* side of the anchor cords. A complete knot involves tying first to the left and then to the right of the anchors.

E. Bring the left over and to the right of the two anchor cords.

F. Place the right cord over the left cord.

G. Pull the right cord through and pull to make . . .

H. . . . the finished knot.

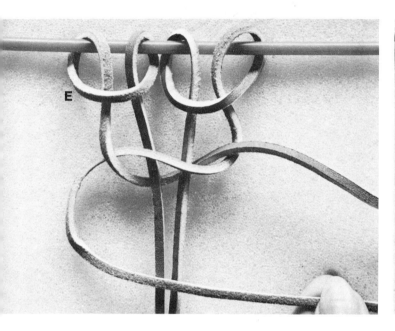

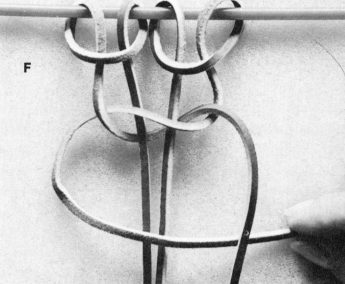

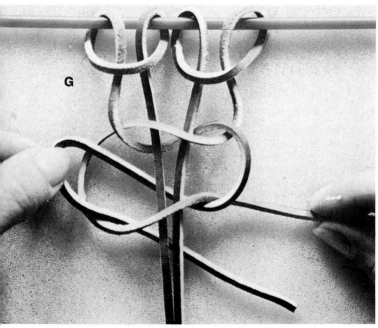

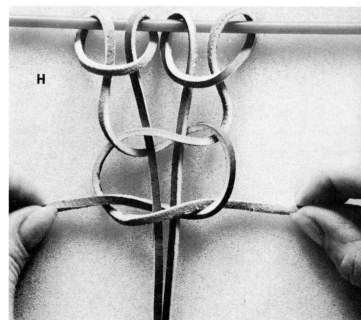

Alternate Square Knot

The alternate square knot is the major variation of square knotting. It is used for belts, jewelry, hangings—any area of macramé. It is simple to follow the procedure for the alternate square knot *(below),* using six cords (twelve strands). Square knot the first row (a) using multiples of four cords for each knot. For the second row (b), drop the first two cords; then continue to square knot with the next multiples of four cords, allowing two loose cords to remain at the end. For the third row (c), pick up the first four cords and continue as in row (a). In the fourth row (d) repeat row (b). Repeat rows (a) and (b) until you achieve the desired length.

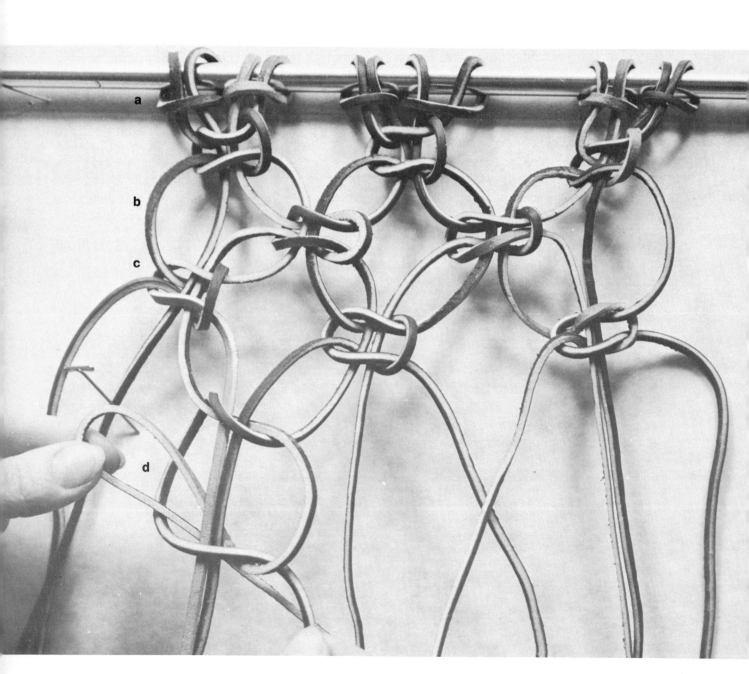

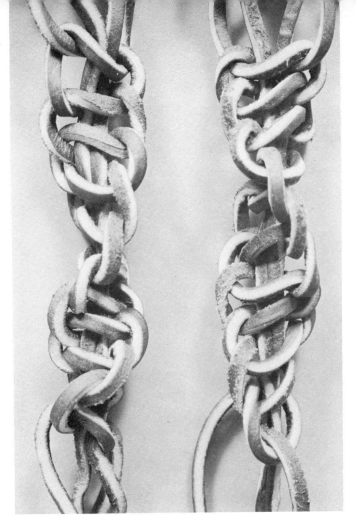

Twisted Sennits

The twisted sennits shown in several of the macramé pieces in this chapter and more specifically in the photo at the left are made by continuously tying only one half of the square knot, resulting in the half knot. When you tie the knot only to one side of the cord, the knots will automatically twist around the anchor. About seven knots are required for a full twist. Knots tied to the left of the anchor will have a left-hand twist. Knots tied only to the right of the anchor will result in a right-hand twist. Twisted lengths may be used straight or crossed over for variety.

Add a bead to the center of a square knot by slipping the bead over the anchor cords after the first half of the tie.

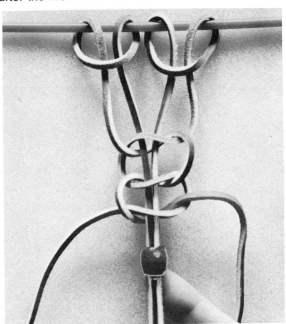

Then complete the second half of the square knot tie to hold the bead.

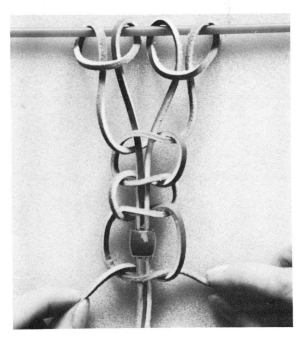

CLOVE HITCH

The clove hitch is the second basic macramé knot after the square knot and may be tied in many directions, progressions, and variations. It consists of tying each strand, in order, over an anchor cord. The knot consists of two loops over the anchor. The lettered illustrations below correspond with the following instructions.

Horizontal Clove Hitch *(tied left to right)*

a. Use the first cord at left for your anchor cord and pin or hold it *taut* horizontally across the board and laid *over* all the knotting strands, which should be smoothed out vertically.

b. Bring the next strand from *under* the anchor cord. Loop it over and around to the left and through the loop as shown. This is the first half of the clove hitch. Tighten the loop.

c. The second half of the knot is made to the right of the first loop. It begins *over* the anchor cord, loops around to the left and through as shown.

d. Make a clove hitch consisting of the two loops illustrated, with each strand worked individually in consecutive

Horizontal clove hitch *(tied left to right).*

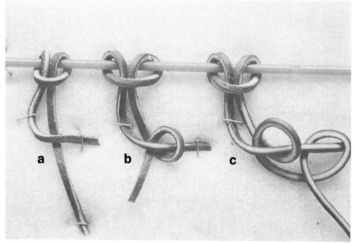

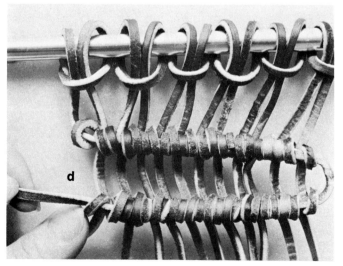

Horizontal clove hitch *(tied right to left).*

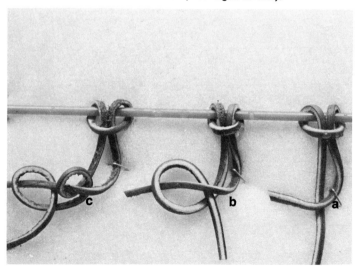

order. The finished row will look like this. If the knots do not look neat, it means you are not holding your anchor cord taut, or you are not pushing each loop onto the cord as it is tied.

Horizontal Clove Hitch *(tied right to left)*

To create a reverse bar, work the clove hitch *right* to *left* using the same anchor cord pinned or held taut across the strands.

a. Hold or pin the anchor cord taut over the knotting strands. Begin knotting with the first strand on the right next to the anchor cord.

b. Loop the knotting strand from *under* the anchor around, over, and through as shown. Tighten.

c. Bring the knotting strand *over* the anchor cord and to the *left* of the first half of the knot for the second loop, working it around and through as shown. Continue to tie each strand individually around the anchor to complete a bar that is knotted from right to left.

d. The finished second bar will look like this. Placement of the anchor any distance from the first bar determines the space between bars.

DIAGONAL BARS

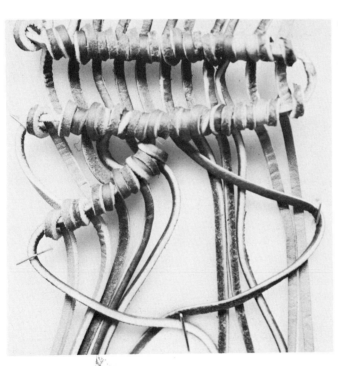

A. Anchor cords may be picked up anywhere in a work to create various patterns and clove hitches, which are knotted over these cords in the necessary direction and in order. To create a diamond shape, pick out the two central cords and pin them diagonally across other strands as shown. Then, beginning from the center, knot each cord over the diagonal using the right-to-left tie for the left side and the left-to-right knot for the other side.

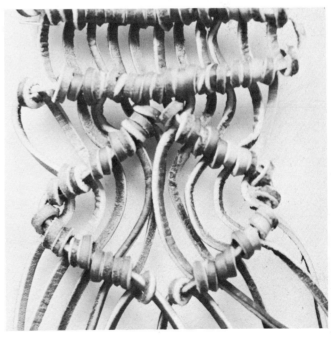

B. The finished diamond shape, knotted with clove hitches. The direction in which the anchor cord is held is the whole secret to clove hitch designs.

NECKLACE. Creative designs by Roberta. Strips of suede show the clove hitch bars, angled clove hitches, and half knot twists.

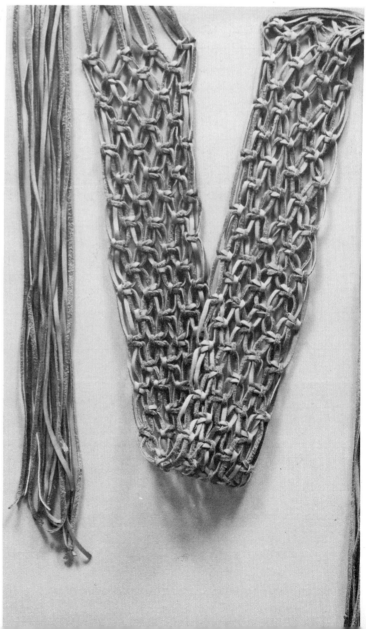

BELT. Creative designs by Roberta. This belt is knotted completely with alternate square knots. Use sixteen 8-foot strips of suede or glove leather. No holding line is used. Allow lengths for fringe, then simply pin the cords to the board. Square knot groups of four strips and continue in the alternating square knot pattern.

NECKLACE. Joyce Barnes. Rawhide lacing was square knotted with seine twine. A collage effect was achieved by cementing and hanging pieces of stone, wood, ceramic beads, cork, and feathers to a solid clove hitched backing.

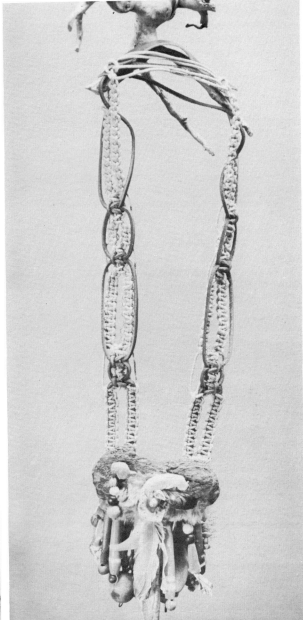

BREAST PLATE . . . NECKPIECE. Susan Meilach. Shapes of 8-ounce cowhide were cut and holes punched in it for connecting the pieces with jute tied in alternate square knots.

SUEDE PURSE WITH KNOTTED FRINGE.
Lynn Doran. During the construction of
the suede purse, strips of suede and
lengths of linen were sewn into the seams
of the flap and bottom. Linen cords
were knotted around the suede strands
and the handle. Seed beads were
added, and fringe was cut to follow
the shape of the purse.

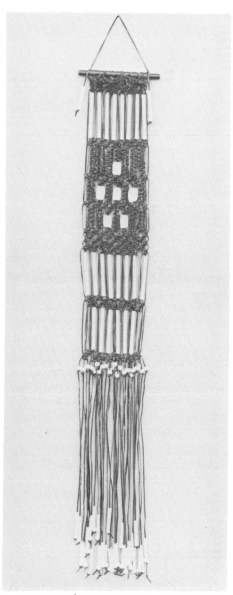

MACRAMÉ HANGING. Neva
Humphreys. Leather lacing was
worked completely in square
knots with beads.

MACRAMÉ NECKPIECE. Dona
Meilach. Skived glove leather
lacing is used for a combination
of the clove hitch and square
knot with beads.

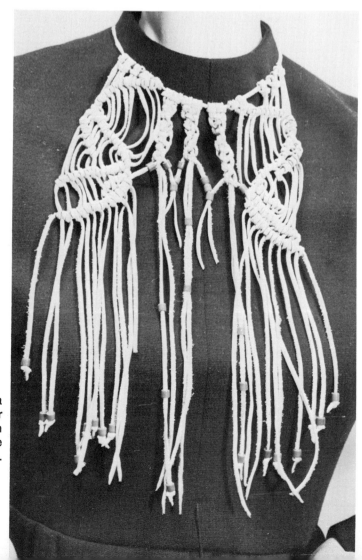

HANGING. Libby Platus. Black-, white-, and
caramel-colored shapes of cowhide and fur pelts are combined
with driftwood, twine, and horsehair and worked with macramé
cords and stitching. PHOTO, VIRGINIA BLACK

KNITTED LEATHER. The suede cape
has knitted leather panels
and lark's head knotted fringe.
The suede pants have knitted side panels,
and the hat is made entirely of knitted
leather. CREATIVE DESIGNS BY ROBERTA

APPLIQUÉ BELTS. Top and bottom
by Gillian Meyers and Freya Biagi;
center two by Frank Stephens. All appliqués
are machine sewn. Cut shapes of various
colored leather are stitched to suede or
cowhide belts. Frank Stephens employs
predesigned appliqués available at
needlework and sewing departments.
PHOTOGRAPHED AT ULTIMO, CHICAGO

CHAPTER TEN

Knitting, Crocheting, Appliquéing

The accompanying designs illustrating knitting and crocheting with soft leather thongs are by Roberta Schmickler of Creative Leathers by Roberta. Roberta has developed the concept of knitting using a pattern of four repeat rows. Knit leather panels laced to solid leather panels are the basis for some of Roberta's unique designs. The remarkable practicality of combining knit and solid panels of leather is that the knitted thongs stretch and reshape themselves thereby making the garments fit almost anyone without bagging and losing their shape.

Roberta's combined knit and solid panels are often edged with a double crochet chain. You may want to try a hat, vest, or other piece of clothing by either crocheting or knitting it entirely. These may be adapted from patterns you would use if working in yarns. Make a size sample to determine the amount of leather you will need, depending on your personal knitting tension. Specific patterns and materials are available from Roberta at her shop in Barrington, Illinois. Leather thongs are sold in various tannery-dyed colors such as red, purple, navy blue, rust, shades of browns, white, grays, and naturals and come in lengths up to 100 feet.

To appliqué leather, you can use a home sewing machine and work the leather much as you would a fabric. However, the toothed foot of a sewing machine tends to push and stretch the bottom layer of thin suede or garment leather as it feeds through the machine, and puckering may occur. Should this happen, you might glue the layer to be appliquéd to the leather base with contact cement and then proceed to stitch, assuming the stitching is part of the decorative design of the piece. For heavier leathers, your home machine may be fitted with a special leather-sewing needle (Singer size 11–16) that has a wedge-shaped point rather than a round one. The wedge-shaped hole made by the needlepoint permits the leather to close up over the thread more efficiently than does a round hole.

Before machine stitching a piece of leather, mark the path of the stitch along a hem or appliqué with a stitching wheel, carefully measuring the distance from the edge with an edge creaser or other suitable instrument. Pretest your machine's ability to stitch on scrap before attempting a seam. No two pieces of suede or leather necessarily react the same to the needle and thread tension and length of stitches. Threads, excluding waxed varieties used

Materials for suede and knitted garments include panels with holes punched for lacing to the knitted panels, a hole punch, scissors, suede thonging, No. 11 or No. 13 aluminum knitting needles, No. F crochet hook, and large eye darning needle.

for hand sewing, are the same as those used for machine sewing, providing they'll feed through the needle and leather.

If you intend to do a great amount of leather appliqué, investigate industrial sewing machines that have a specially designed

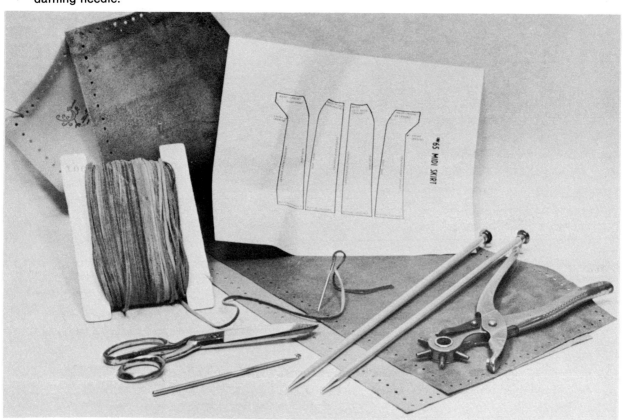

A knitted panel has tremendous elasticity. Here you see the pattern from the right side after it has been carefully laced into the holes along the sides of the solid leather panels.

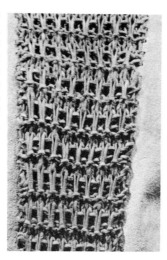

The inside of the garment illustrates how simple it is to attach the knitted leather panel to the underside of the punched solid piece with a running stitch that does not show on the topside.

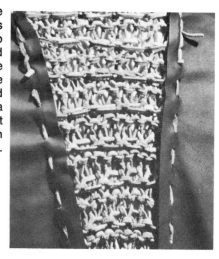

foot-feed mechanism that pushes both top and bottom leather pieces through simultaneously without stretching them. These machines may be purchased secondhand, or your shoemaker or any local leather craftsman may help you locate a possible source.

Machine stitching is also used for making leather handbags, watchbands, shoes, and a variety of other things. If you plan to do a great amount of leatherwork, an industrial sewing machine might be a worthwhile investment.

Procedure for knitting involves casting on an odd number of stitches in the same way that you cast on for yarn knitting. Begin with a loop, then loop and knot the stitch onto the needle.

For row one: knit one stitch, then slip one stitch as if to purl. Then, repeat across the row, ending with knit one.

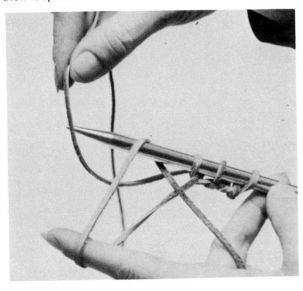

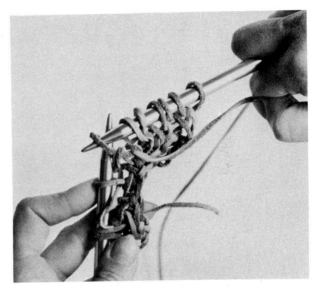

Row two: knit one, pass yarn to front of work, slip one stitch, pass yarn to back of work, then knit one. Repeat across the row from the point at which you pass yarn to front of work and end with knit one.

Knit rows three and four. Then, repeat the series of four rows. After you complete each row, pull down on the work to shape your knitted design.

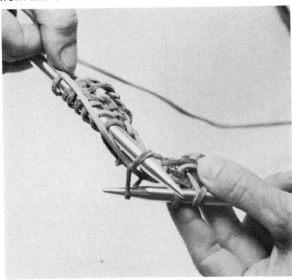

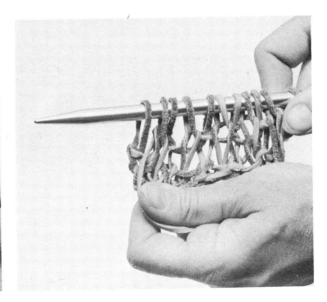

VEST. Creative Leathers by
Roberta. Panels of suede are
stitched to panels of knitting.
The edges are crocheted.

Rear view of vest at left.

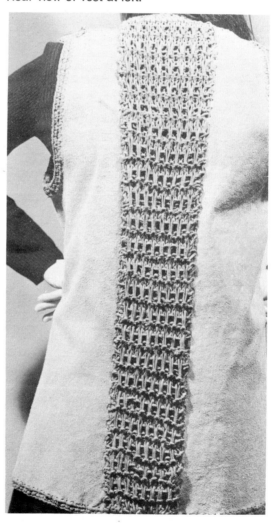

ALL-KNITTED JERKIN.
Creative Leathers by Roberta.

HIP HUGGER PANTS. Creative
Leathers by Roberta.

KNITTED AND CROCHETED HATS. Creative Leathers by Roberta.

By applying needlecraft techniques to leather, Roberta has also pioneered the use of French knots as a decorative and joining stitch for a belt and pouch.

The French knot is made by bringing the needle up from the bottom to the top of the fabric, winding the leather thong around the base of the needle three times, then punching the needle back down through the same hole. As the thong is pulled, it will automatically create the decorative knot.

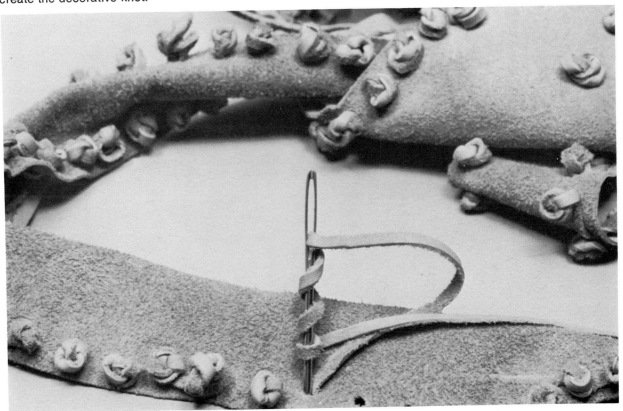

DETAILS OF APPLIQUÉ BELTS *(shown in color photo at the beginning of this chapter).*

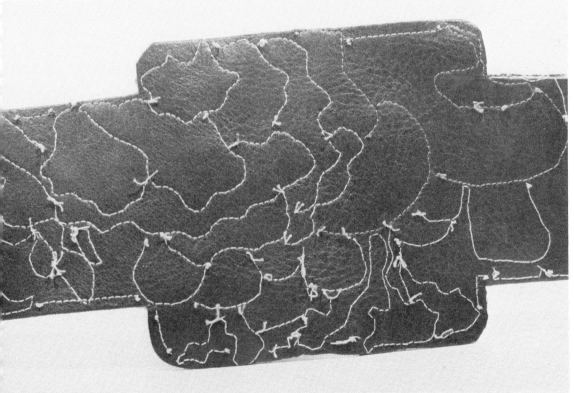

Map-like paths of stitches on back of belt above are shown. Each top and bottom set of threads is square knotted to prevent loosening.

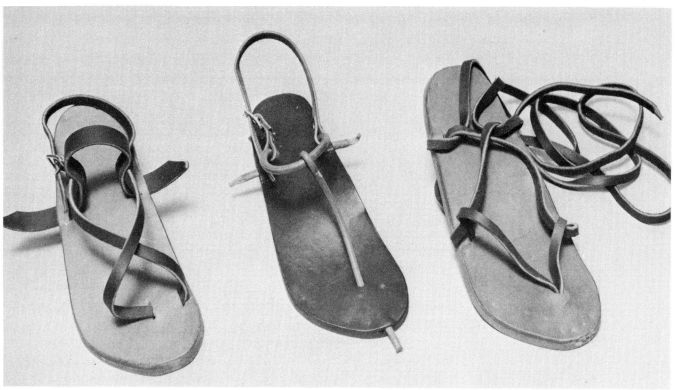

TOE THONG SANDALS. Murry Kusmin. Three different styles of
toe thong sandals with wet molded arches are shown. Straps
protrude because they are cut to length only after they are
custom fitted. Then, they are cobbled and edge finished.

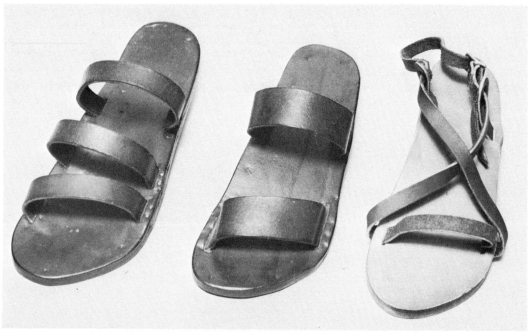

STRAP SANDALS. Murry Kusmin. Strap leather may be
prestretched by wetting and pulling it before
cementing it into the soles.

CHAPTER ELEVEN

Sandalmaking

Why make your own sandals when you can buy manufactured sandals from thousands of shoe stores? The answer is tied in with the whole movement of individual creativity—the desire to make something with your own hands. The concept of a handmade, custom-fitted pair of sandals is enticing. You can use the finest leather and develop your own styles and colors. The cost of materials is minimal, and the sandals probably will wear longer than any mass-produced pair.

Among sandalmakers, there are differing opinions as to how sandals should be made. Six different sandalmakers will have six varying theories, and all of them valid. Some prefer a greater use of cobbling nails; some insist stitching should be used; some prefer setting in shanks and arch supports; some make soles that are flat; others mold the arch; some swear that heels are necessary; others use no heels. Even the practice of finishing edges differs: some leave corners squared off; others bevel them. Straps, too, are open to different approaches. One sandalmaker prefers industrial belting, another latigo, still another stripped cowhide.

Regardless of individual differences among craftsmen, none are right or wrong:

it's all a matter of preference. But the general thinking behind sandalmaking is that one should strive for comfortable fit, long wear, and good design.

Historical evidence points to the fact that sandals were among the first applications for leather and probably the first footwear. Florida sandalmaker Dan Holiday traces the early history of sandals and leather tanning in his delightful booklet, *The Sandal Fitting*. He tells how earliest man fastened a hard piece of rawhide around each foot for protection. In Egyptian tombs carved stone tablets show that sandals were worn. Tomb wall paintings at Thebes illustrate the process of sandalmaking and the preparation of leather, which was very similar to present tanning methods.

There is also evidence, says Mr. Holiday, that "Egyptian sandalmakers had to cater to fashion. The aristocracy, and women generally, wore a sandal with a turned up toe; the lower classes wore sandals with a rounded or pointed toe."

Ancient sandal styles, illustrated in various encyclopedias, may serve as inspiration for contemporary styling. Studying manufactured sandals also will give you some insight into designs, strap placement, and

CUSTOM DESIGNED SANDALS. Dan Holiday. All of these sandals have heels that are laminated and are attached to the sole by cobbling (from top and bottom) and cementing. In sandals designed with heels, Mr. Holiday often uses a metal arch shank for support. Here you see a top *(above)* and side view *(below)* of the same sandals.

styles. The genuine satisfaction is to design a comfortable sandal that is unique.

To make sandals, you will need at least two kinds of leather. For bottom soles use a 9–14 iron, combination chrome- and vegetable-tanned sole leather. Sole leather is measured in "irons" rather than ounces as is cowhide. Iron measures range from No. .75, which is about 1/64 of an inch thick, to No. 14, which is about 1/4 of an inch thick. You can buy sole leather from shoe-maker suppliers and, possibly, from your neighborhood shoemaker. It may be precut to sole sizes or may come in sheets that can be cut to your own sole shapes.

Top soles should be made from vege-table-tanned, 5- to 9-ounce uncolored shoulder cowhide if you are going to wet the leather and mold the sandal. (If you are not going to wet the leather for molding, coloring is not so important.) Cowhide isn't always wet molded because it is soft and will conform to the foot's shape. You also will need full or top grain strap leather. Major prerequisites for strap leather are that it does not stretch too much and is soft or may be softened by rubbing or immersing in neat's-foot oil.

In the accompanying illustrations Murry Kusmin demonstrates how to make wet-molded toe thong sandals finished by cob-bling. With these basic instructions many variations are possible. When selecting strap findings such as rings or buckles avoid those with sharp edges or protrusions that might cut the feet and ankles.

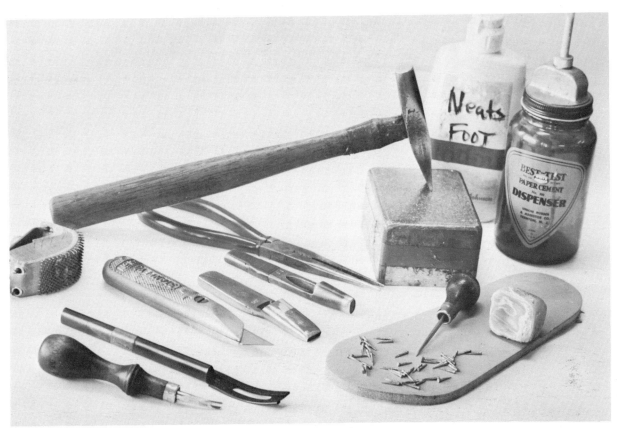

Tools for making sandals include a cobbler's hammer and anvil (a solid metal surface to strike the nail point against), cutting tools, edge beveler, skive, slot and oval drive punches, needle nose pliers, rasp, awl, clinching nails, beeswax, cement, and neat's-foot oil. You will also need Scotch tape, water, dyes for coloring, and a wheel for sanding and buffing.

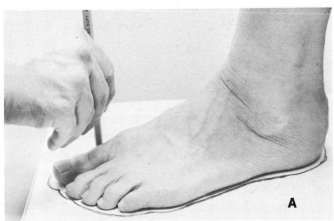

A. Make a cardboard pattern of each foot. Mark the beginning and end of the arch, the spot between the big toe and second toe, and the placement of the side strap about one-third of the distance from the end of the heel. Mark the pattern "left" and "right" and indicate "top" on each.

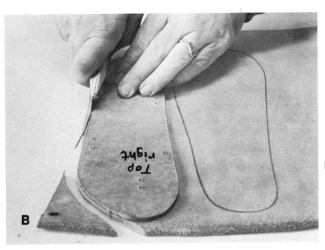

B. Transfer the pattern to the upper sole cowhide, allowing about ¼ inch extra edge for working. This edge will be trimmed later. Use the cut top sole to make the bottom sole pattern. Be sure to reverse the bottom sole so you don't have two negatives that won't fit together.

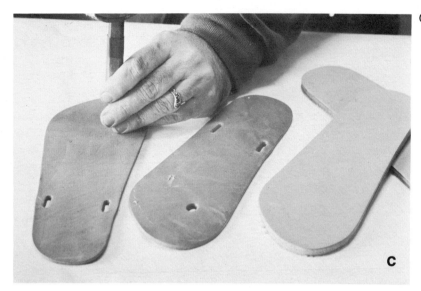

C

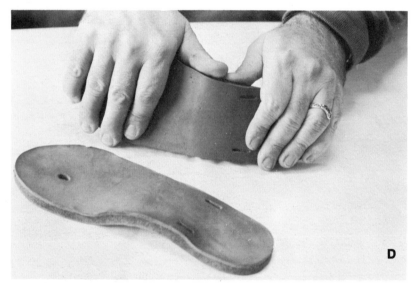

D

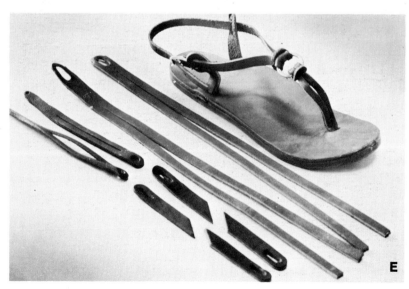

E

C. With all four soles cut, punch the necessary strap and toe holes in the top soles only, far enough in from the edge to allow for trimming and finishing and for the nails to hold in the strap. Use your awl or a pencil to mark the shape of the arch. Straps properly located toward the back end of the arch will prevent the heel strap from slipping. Note that straps are not put in until *after* the soles are laminated and molded. Next, laminate the top and bottom soles with contact cement and place the roughened flesh sides together. Before adhering the soles, lay a strip of Scotch tape from the edge to each punched strap hole. This produces an unglued path so that later the straps can be placed without prying open and tearing the leather layers. Dry the glued soles at least 24 hours before molding.

D. To wet mold the arch, dip the dried, laminated soles in warm water for 5 to 10 minutes, depending upon how pliable you want it to be for bending and pushing. Using your arch mark as your guide, hold the sole as shown. Place your thumbs along the edge to be curved and work the wet leather to the arch shape. Curve the end of the heel and bend the top up slightly. Again, set aside the soles to dry at least 24 hours. When dry, test comfort of the arch. Remold the arch if necessary and dry thoroughly. Then rub or dip the soles in neat's-foot oil to restore the oils lost during wetting. Also do preliminary dyeing and edge beveling and sanding before putting in the straps.

E. Cut straps about ½ inch wide and 2 to 3 inches longer than necessary, stripping them from hide with a stripper, paper cutter, or shears. Use latigo or 4- to 6-ounce top or full grain cowhide rubbed with neat's-foot oil to make the straps soft and flexible. Make the necessary strap punches and slits where straps will slip through one another.

F. Now, open path between soles where tape is and pull each strap through beyond edge of sandal. If you have inadvertently glued the soles completely together, open up the path by prying with a screwdriver. When all straps are pulled through, skive ends, then try on sandal and fit straps to your foot. Then cobble, or nail, soles and straps together. If you use a minimum of nails and the straps do stretch, you can always remove the nails, adjust straps, and cobble again.

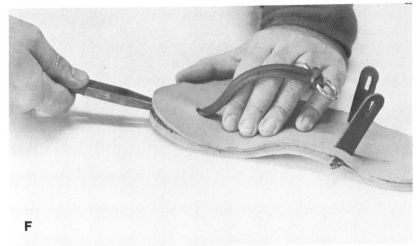

F

G. To cobble, use a triangular-shaped pointed clinching nail that is a little longer than the thickness of all leathers because the end is bent over when hammered against the anvil. Brass and steel nails come in ⅜ to 1¼ inch lengths. A ⅝-inch brass nail is used here. Nail from the bottom to the top of the sole. Later, this will prevent a worn nail from poking into your foot. Punch a starting hole with your awl, set the nail in, and nail, holding the top of the sole flat against a hard iron anvil. For nailing, the head of a regular hammer probably will do, and a piece of pipe or gear might serve as an anvil. As you nail, the nail tip will bend over and back into the top sole and won't protrude. Cobble all strap areas. Some sandalmakers cobble all around the sole from the top to the bottom at 1-inch intervals.

G

H. To finish sandals, trim off any excess edge, taking care not to trim too close to strap holes and cobbler's nails. Bevel the top and bottom edges of the sandal if you like. Immerse the sandal in neat's-foot oil for about 10 minutes. Finish edges by additional beveling; sanding; waxing; burnishing with beeswax, water, or saddle soap; and buffing. Wear sandals only 3 to 4 hours for the first few days.

H

CAPE AND MATCHING DRESS.
Paul Luckey, Pegasus Unique
Leather Creations, Sausalito,
Calif. This buckskin ensemble
has a hooded cape trimmed in
turkey feathers.

Rear view. Hood becomes
deep, feather-trimmed
collar.

CHAPTER TWELVE

Clothing

Leather is becoming increasingly popular as a material for skirts, pants, vests, coats, capes, ponchos, hats and other wearing apparel. With the endless array of styles for men and women of every age it would be impossible to present a thorough discussion of clothing in terms of leather styling, assembling, and sewing in one short chapter.

It has been elected, therefore, to present the basic procedures and techniques for leather pattern selection and assemblage that can be applied to any pattern you may wish to make. For demonstration we have shown a simple method for creating a leather vest. For more advanced approaches to making leather clothes refer to any book on general sewing techniques and specifically to the book *How to Sew Leather, Suede and Fur* by Schwebke and Krohn. Also, many pattern companies now have developed styles that can be made from either woven fabric or leather. Your yard goods supplier also may recommend leather patterns.

Another approach is to use a pattern taken from a garment you already have, or to design a pattern yourself. The wisest procedure is to make a paper pattern, then pretest it on a piece of muslin or old sheet cut to the same size as the hide to determine the best way for cutting the leather. (See Chapter 2 for yardage estimating.)

When you buy garment leather or suede, it's good practice to take your pattern with you and lay it out on the skin. First to make sure that you buy enough leather, and second to see that imperfections such as thin spots or holes in the skin will not fall at critical parts of the garment.

Skins have grain that runs lengthwise from head to tail. Pattern pieces placed *with* the grain on either the hide or flesh side usually drape more satisfactorily.

Seams, darts, facings, and hems in leather may be glued with a flexible glue such as a contact cement or white glue. They may be sewn by hand or machine or laced. (See Chapter 10 for machine sewing.) If leathers stretch or slip while sewing, lightly glue or tape the seam allowance. After the seam is made, open the allowance and crease the edges back with a rubber mallet or bone creaser. When machine sewing, always tie the threads at the end of a line. Do not back sew or the double stitching will show.

Garment leather is usually of 3- to 4-ounce weight and can come from many animals other than a cow. There are elkskin, buckskin, and deerskin, antelope, and many others. Suede, readily available at

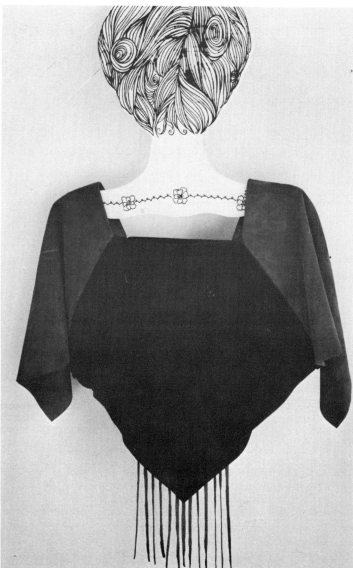

VEST AND PONCHO. Jack De Carolis. These items are easy for the beginner to create, and Mr. De Carolis demonstrates techniques for making them in the following series of photos.

many sewing counters or leather suppliers, is a good choice for a beginner. Precut fringe in several colors is also available and comes by the yard like drapery and curtain trim. Trim may be glued or sewn to solid pieces of leather as opposed to being cut from the original length. In this way, you don't have to buy such a large piece of leather to allow for the trim, and you have less waste. When working with suede, be sure to lay out the pieces so the nap of the grain is matched, giving an all over even shading to the entire garment. Ordinary sharp household scissors, a leather cutting shears, razor blade, or knife may be used for cutting garment leathers.

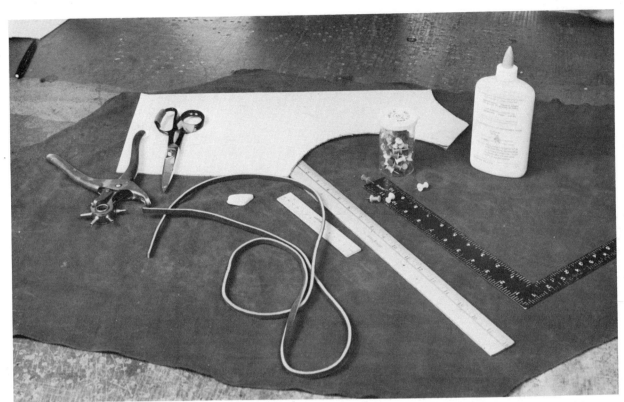

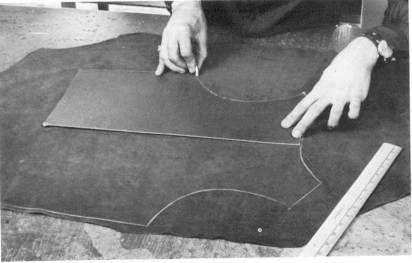

Materials for making a three-piece vest having a back and two front panels include a pattern (transferred from tissue to cardboard to make it stiff), scissors, hole punch, ruler, pins, glue, skin, and lacing.

Place the pattern along the grain of the leather. Do not fold leather in half to cut as you would a fabric, but simply flip the pattern over at the middle and draw the second half. The bottom of the pattern is extended to allow for fringing. However, an alternative is to buy precut fringe and to add it by gluing or sewing.

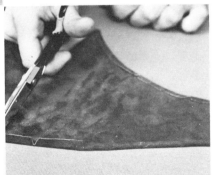

A curved seam allowance should be clipped in a wedge shape to allow for stretching.

Glue edge hem with white glue or rubber cement. Crease and press firmly with fingers or bone creaser. Pound the edge with a rubber mallet.

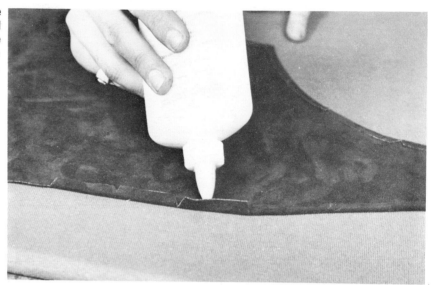

Measure and mark the placement of holes to be used for lacing and cut with revolving punch. This vest will be laced together rather than sewn or glued. Cross lacing will be used at the shoulders and sides for joining and added detail. This entire vest may be created without sewing.

Lace the seams together. Here the bottom has been fringed by cutting the leather with a razor using a steel straight edge as a guide.

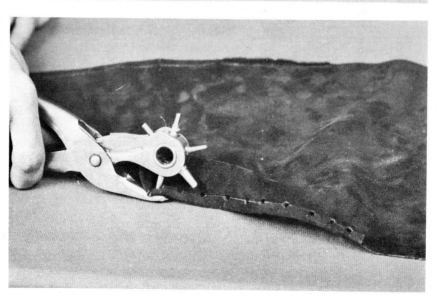

Belts may be made by cutting, gluing, and lacing. These belts will be tied; no buckles are needed.

Poncho made with double stitched seams and eyelets to hold lacing secured with beads.

LEATHER PANTS.
Jack De Carolis.

PURSES. Jack De Carolis. Using suede or garment leather and the same techniques as those shown for vests, you can make soft purses in a variety of styles. No sewing is required. Only designing, planning, cutting, and gluing.

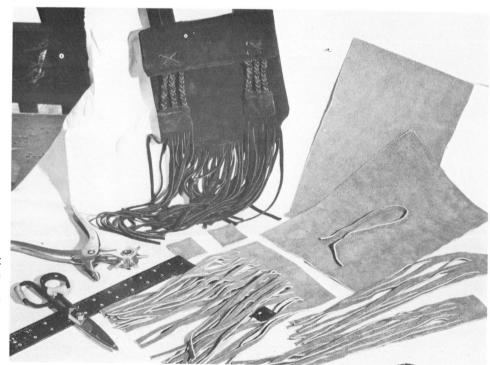

To make the purse at left *(above),* the component parts are: two solid and one partially fringed rectangle, four narrow fringed bands, small squares for attaching the braided bands, and a double thick band for the handle.

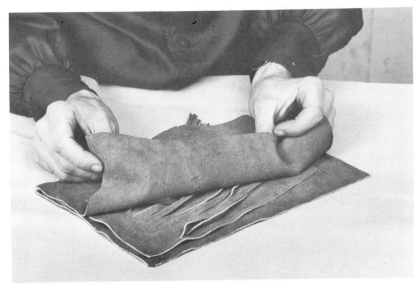

Place the fringed rectangle between the left sides of the solid rectangles and glue all edges except the right *(top)* edge in the photo so that the fringe will protrude from the bottom when purse is inverted.

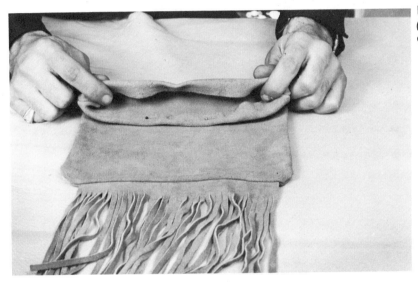

Invert the purse, fold the flap *(top),* and pin the flap edge under.

Insert one narrow band of fringe at each side of flap, lace through and glue, then braid. Add fringe at bottom to both the right and left front of the purse, then connect the ends of braid to top of fringe and cover with a small rectangle. Glue flap hem, glue handles.

STEPPENWOLF. Pat Swenson. Loom woven piece with yarn, sheep's wool, and suede strips.   PHOTO, RICHARD EELLS

CHAPTER THIRTEEN

Potpourri

In working with many artists and leather-workers around the country, leather being used in ways that did not fall into any specific category, such as sculpture, collage, and clothing, was discovered. Hence, this chapter, titled "Potpourri," is meant to serve as an additional idea stimulator. Whether you make your living from leather or work with it occasionally, you may discover ideas here that you can use directly or with other media and techniques.

Perhaps one of the most dominant applications of leather in mixed media statements is weaving it on looms or frames and combining it with fur strips and with other fibers. Such weavings, which reach an extremely high artistic and practical level, are represented in the work of Pat Swenson of Milwaukee, Wisconsin. In her weavings she uses wide and narrow leather strips and bands for both warp and weft. The textures that result are equally successful whether wall hangings, capes, or ponchos.

Leather strips and free-form shapes are used in woven rugs made by Lynn Doran. Strips of suede and garment leather added measurably to the rich textured surfaces that Henry Stahmer achieved in his hooked and punched rugs and wall hangings. Mr. Stahmer also glues flat free-form leather shapes onto canvas backgrounds, then stitches over portions to achieve exquisite creative stitcheries.

George Thiewes wraps and stitches pieces of suede around hand-blown glass bottles to create sculptural forms—an unusual combination of media.

Chess pieces by John Anderson, himself a chess buff, are designed as sculpture, yet each piece retains its identity in the game. The chessmen are made with laminating and winding techniques using cowhide and sole leather.

Pieces of suede can be made into stuffed animals, but the ultimate in toys might be Bruce Vetter's leather car. Mr. Vetter admits that it would be economically unfeasible to market this toy—it took him fourteen hours to create it.

Leather jewelry and body adornments are a natural in combination with other organic, handmade, and manufactured objects. John Cederquist and Ernest Kramer combine hanks of hair and pieces of bone in their fetish jewelry inspired by African and Indian artifacts. Sandrayvonne Baker developed a chest bib by thinking in terms of covering the body with sculpture. Joyce Barnes uses shells, ceramics, and twine with fur, leather, and rawhide in her necklaces.

Techniques presented for working leather may be applied to any end. The object is to be inventive, experimental, and innovative. Leather is a medium with many moods and properties still to be creatively explored.

CHESS SET. John Anderson. Unusually designed leather chess sets are as sculptural as they are practical. This set is made of laminated 12-ounce sole leather, finely finished and edged. Shapes are ingeniously planned to fit, jigsaw-puzzle fashion, into the specially designed leather carrying box.

CHESS SET AND BOARD. John Anderson. Strips of 5-ounce vegetable-tanned leather are dipped in water and wound to create this chess set. After winding the wet leather, Mr. Anderson allows it to dry; then he unwinds it carefully, coats the surfaces with Barge cement, and rewinds to hold permanently. The board is made of two layers of 2-ounce cowhide, which is laminated for extra strength. Ends are "tooled" by using the edge of a hammer head on the wet leather. The entire piece is dyed; edges are finished and rubbed with beeswax. Final oiling, polishing, and buffing are accomplished.

LARGE CHESS SET. John Anderson. Each piece in this set is about 4 inches high. This height allows the pieces to take on an architectural quality. For the larger diameter of these pieces, John Anderson incorporates a ½-inch wood dowel as a core in the length of the bottom portion of the piece. The wood is stained the same color as the playing piece.

Detail of the chess pieces illustrates how leather is wound over wood dowel cores. Each piece is glued entirely; the outside ends are tacked for extra holding strength.

WOVEN RUG. Lynn Doran. Wool, jute, and suede strips
woven on a loom.   COURTESY, ARTIST

WALL HANGING IN
PROGRESS (detail).
Henry Stahmer. Jagged
patches of leather are
glued to canvas back-
ing, and stitchery is
used over them. Thin
leather and felt strips
are hooked through
backing between flat
leather shapes.

LEATHER ELEPHANT. Richard Blackwell.
Using patterns from old-fashioned calico
cloth animals, Mr. Blackwell developed
a series of oversized stuffed animals
with sole leather feet. They are stuffed
with foam rubber granules.

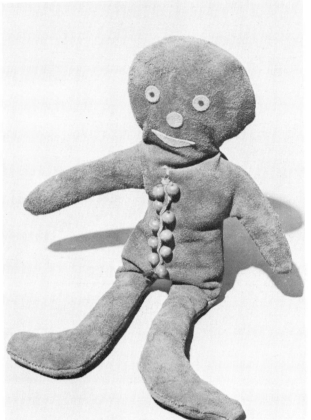

LEATHER DOLL. Linda Vetter. Practically
indestructible, this doll is the modern
interpretation of Raggedy Ann.

ROADSTER, Bruce Vetter.
This purple leather model has
shaped hood, laced "welds,"
and laminated wheels that
turn on metal axles.

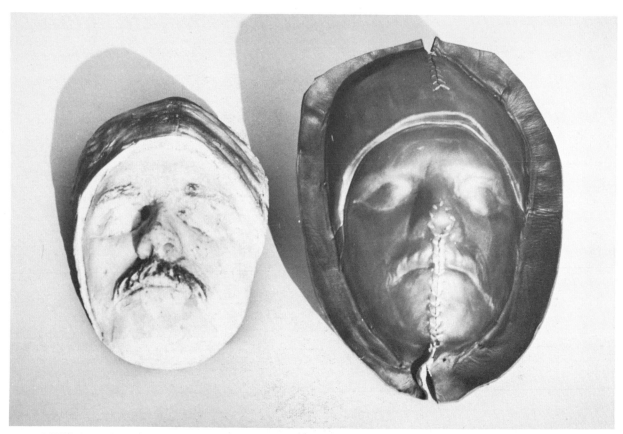

ACTUAL FACE MASK OF THE ARTIST. Bruce Vetter. The formed leather mask was made over a plaster mold taken from the artist's face. If you try this, vaseline your face thoroughly before applying plaster and insert a straw in your nostrils for breathing while plaster hardens.

If you have a leather shop or work corner, you might use cutouts for a sign and develop a logo of leather.

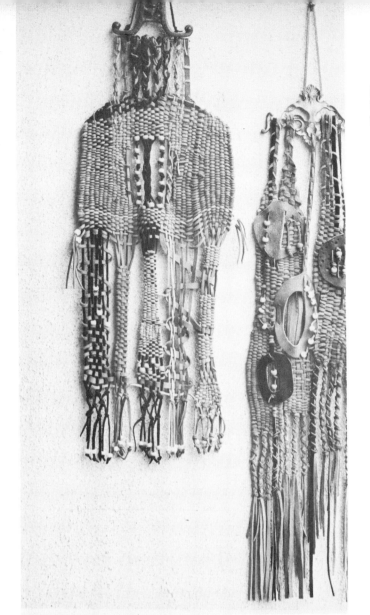

NON-LOOM WEAVING. Lynn Doran. Leather and felt strips are used in woven shapes.

BLOWN GLASS BOTTLE, LEATHER COVER. George Thiewes. A beautiful wedding of unlike materials.

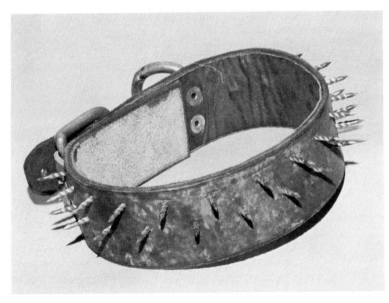

DOG COLLAR. Bruce Vetter. To protect his dog, which seemed to be the scapegoat of every vicious dog in the neighborhood, Bruce Vetter designed a dog collar that has the appearance of a torture rack . . . but it did the trick.

JEWELRY. Truman Xavier Jones. Many traditional leather findings are employed in modern designs including cartridge holders, which are used here on a dog-collar necklace, bracelets, watchbands, and pendant necklaces. A variety of unusual findings have been adapted from sources other than leatherwork suppliers.

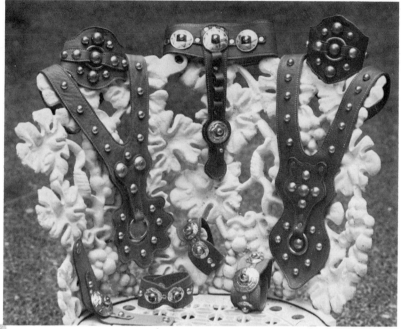

NECKLACE. Robert Henion. Carefully designed shapes of leather are the backing for dangling parts that actually are railroad spikes; the flat shapes are also found objects and are fastened to the leather with eyelets.

NKYIMKYIM CHEST BIB. Sandrayvonne Baker. Twisted and knotted leather thongs are combined with brass rings within and at the ends. PHOTO, BILAL

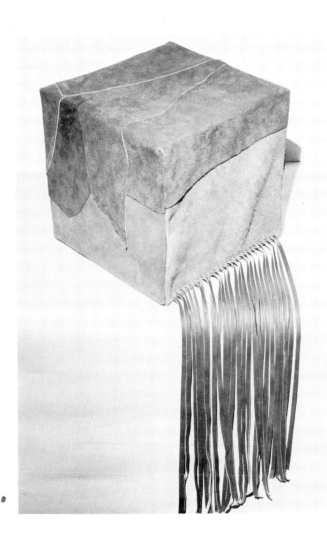

CUBE. Dan Kovacevic. A cube covered with shapes of leather and fringed at one end was a graduate degree project in art using leather in three-dimensional form.

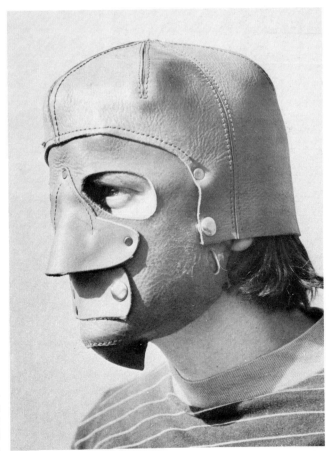

MASK. Bruce Vetter. This snap-apart mask was designed for cold weather motorcycling. Its various snap openings, with head and jaw pieces that open up on hinges, are reminiscent of ancient armor.

LARGO. Ernest Kramer. 27 in. high, 22 in. wide. Fetish necklace having leather fringe and neckpiece, pounded and flattened brass rods, calf ribs, turkey vertebrae, and herring gull feather.

FETISH NECKPIECE. John Cederquist. Leather shapes are combined with wrapped twigs, bamboo, feathers, and fur.

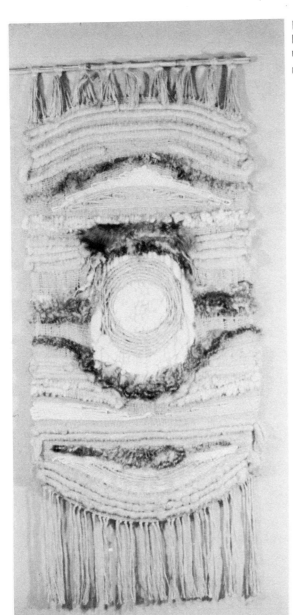

LOOM WOVEN WALL HANGING. Pat Swenson.
Heavy yarns and strips of leather are
used in this weaving.

PHOTO, RICHARD EELLS

CYLINDRICAL WEAVING. Pat Swenson.
Fur, feathers, leather strips, and heavy
yarns are used to give a free-form,
three-dimensional quality
to this hanging.

PHOTO, RICHARD EELS

CHAIR. Ed Stiles. Walnut and leather.

CHAPTER FOURTEEN

Furniture

To complete an overall view of artistic applications of leather, it is essential to show some of its uses in contemporary furniture design. Admittedly, one has to know how to work with wood, metal, or plastic to use leather in furniture, but many craftsmen work with many media. The furniture selected for this chapter is both functional and artistically designed. The pieces have a genuine sculptural quality by virtue of the frame design; they exist in space and are successful and pleasing from every angle and side. These pieces also reveal an expressive approach by their creators, who have beautifully integrated materials and form.

Each of the pieces illustrated was made by the craftsman for his own use, and many merited exhibition at the Pasadena Art Museum design shows. Some designs have been purchased for manufacturing.

In addition to appreciating the craftsmanship involved and design problems solved in each of the illustrated works, you may be inspired to make your own furniture. There are no specific or absolute procedures for making original furniture. Instructions presented for making leather projects throughout the book are equally applicable here—combined with good taste, design, sound structuring, and comfort.

You also might consider using leather for renewing existing furniture. It's amazing what can be done by slinging a leather seat across an old chair that may have originally had webbing and a cushion, or renewing an old rocker or captain's chair with a leather seat and back. Leather may be wrapped around a wood spindle and nailed. Or a spindle may be grooved horizontally, the leather inserted, and a screw put through both wood and leather and held with a wood peg of the same or a contrasting wood. It is possible to use upholstery techniques with leather, and, of course, upholstered leather furniture has been on the market for years. Leather upholstered items are expensive, but finding suitable hides and reupholstering an old chair or couch is not an insurmountable task although it does require motivation.

Additional ideas for leather furniture may be gleaned from furniture stores, especially those carrying Mexican, Italian, Spanish, and Scandinavian styles. Import shops carry lines of leather items from around the world and can spark imaginative ideas for leather usage. These shops also sell furs and hides that can be used for area rugs. Furs often make interesting cushions for leather chairs, too.

Leather may be applied to wood furniture as a veneer. It is particularly beautiful on desk tops, end tables, cube tables—wherever the richness of leather is desired. Always be sure a furniture surface is clean and smooth before bonding leather. Cut the leather accurately and finish visible edges before adhering. Leather furniture may be highlighted with stains or paint and decorated with traditional or modern tooled designs.

ROCKER. Roger Douglas Collins.
Birchwood frame, leather sling.
COURTESY, PASADENA ART MUSEUM, CALIF.,
PHOTO, RICHARD GROSS

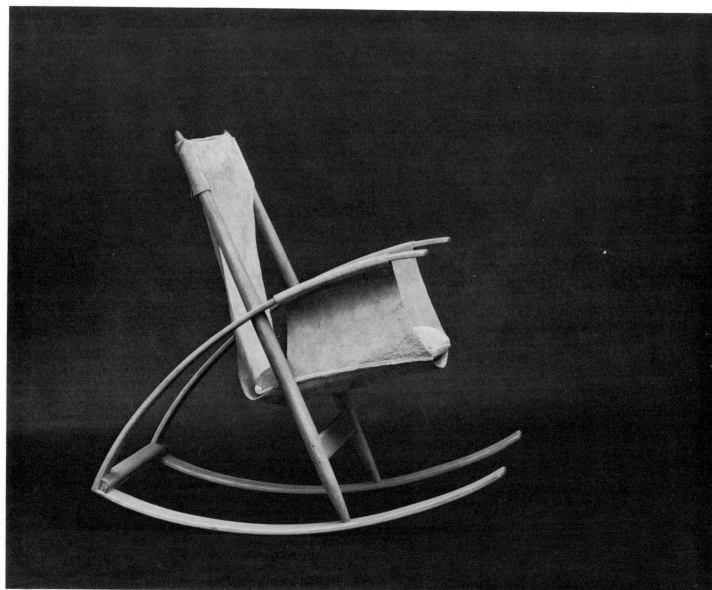

SIDE CHAIR. Lawrence Hunter.
Cherry and live-oak leather chair
has a seat attached in grooves
and held in place with
wooden pegs.
COURTESY, ARTIST

ROCKER. Lawrence Hunter. Oak
wood, live-oak leather and
goatskin cushions. Leather is
attached by first dampening it
to shape it to the contour of
the wood, then gluing it
with white glue.
COURTESY, ARTIST

CHAIR. Lawrence Hunter.
Front view of chair on
opposite page.

Detail of construction of
chair on opposite page
shows how leather seat is
cut and held at rear. Knobs
adjust tension of seat.

ALL PHOTOS, COURTESY, ARTIST

CHAIR. Lawrence Hunter. The vegetable-tanned leather was cut, dampened, and formed to the cherry wood frame and secured by gluing the edges into wood slits.

ROOM DIVIDER OR SCREEN. Murry Kusmin. The negative area remaining from cut straps, belts, panels, and shoe soles have been inserted into this attractive wooden-framed screen.

FIBER GLASS ROCKER.
Lawrence Hunter. This
piece has a ramskin
fur seat.

NOBLE OAK AND
LEATHER CHAIR.
John Snidecor.

COURTESY, PASADENA
ART MUSEUM, CALIF.,
PHOTO, RICHARD GROSS

Supply Sources

The following sources for materials and tools will help you get started working with leather. For a complete listing of tanners, write to the American Tanners Association, 411 Fifth Avenue, New York, New York 10016. For additional sources, begin your research in the classified pages of the telephone book for the urban center nearest you or in the Thomas Registry at your local library. Look for leather distributors and jobbers, leather finding companies, tanners, shoe findings companies, etc. If you are seeking buckles, buttons, rivets, etc., look under "findings" for jewelry, handbags, shoes. (See Chapter 2.) Send a postcard to the Shoe Service Institute of America, 222 W. Adams Street, Chicago, Illinois 60606, for an up-to-date listing of leather and allied materials sources.

Many tools and supplies of listed manufacturers are available locally in hardware stores and craft shops. If you don't have a supplier near you where you can personally select hides, they may be ordered by mail from the sources listed here.

By sending a postcard to one or more of the listed sources, you usually will receive a catalog or price list or be referred to a local distributor. Listings are for ordering convenience and are based on recommendations by the artists whose works appear in the book. No endorsements or guarantees are implied.

LEATHER IN SMALL AMOUNTS, SPECIAL ORDERS, AND MISCELLANEOUS SUPPLIES

A. C. Products
422 Hudson Street
New York, N.Y. 10001

Amber Leather Co.
835 San Julian
Los Angeles, Calif. 90052
Scrap leather sold by the pound

Bergman Leather Co.
103 South Street
Boston, Mass. 02109
Shoe soling and leathers

Ira Berman
147 South Street
Boston, Mass. 02109
Leather

John Cirardi
259 Bleeker Street
New York, N.Y. 10000
Scrap and tools

Drake Leather Co.
3500 West Beverly Blvd.
Montebello, Calif. 90640

D. D. Holiday & Co.
15 St. George Street
St. Augustine, Fla. 32084

J. C. Larson Co., Inc.
7330 N. Clark Street
Chicago, Ill. 60626
Supplies for schools and tools

Mac Leather
424 Broome Street
New York, N.Y. 10013

MacPherson Bros.
730 Polk Street
San Francisco, Calif. 94100
Leather and tools

Roberta Creative Leathers
296 Donlea
Barrington, Ill. 60010
Knitting and macramé thongs; precut designs

Sax Arts & Crafts
207 N. Milwaukee
Milwaukee, Wis. 53202
Skins, lacing, tools

M. Siegel Co., Inc.
114 South Street
Boston, Mass. 02111

Tandy
Mail and local retail outlets
Check classified for local stores
Leather tools, dyes, glues

The Tannery
49 Grove Street
New York, N.Y. 10001
Leather, tools

Lee Ward
840 North State
Elgin, Ill. 60120

LEATHER TANNERS

Allied Kid Co.
209 South Street
Boston, Mass. 02111
*Cattle and kip, side and patent, suede splits,
goat and kid, upper, lining,
glove and garment*

Armour Leather Co.
1113 Maryland Avenue
Sheboygan, Wis. 53082
Kip, side, upper, specialty, splits, lining

Beggs & Cobb, Inc.
171 Madison Avenue
New York, N.Y. 10016
Reptile

W. D. Byron & Sons, Inc.
Williamsport, Md. 21795

Granite State Leather Co., Inc.
Fairmount Street
Nashua, N.H. 03060

Gran Tanning Corp.
Milton Mills, N.H. 03852

Irving Tanning Co., Inc.
134 Beach Street
Boston, Mass. 02111

A. C. Lawrence Leather Co.
10 Sawyer Street
Peabody, Mass. 01961

McAdoo & Allen Welting Co., Inc.
Quakertown, Bucks County, Pa. 18951

Middleburg Tanning Corp.
351 North 3rd Street
Philadelphia, Pa. 19106

Modern Leather Co., Inc.
11–15 Spring Street
Peabody, Mass. 01961

North & Judd
New Britain, Conn. 06050

Fred Rueping Leather Co., Inc.
Fond du Lac, Wis. 54936

Scholze Tannery, Inc.
3100 St. Elmo Avenue
Chattanooga, Tenn. 37402

Seal Tanning Co., Inc.
Commercial Street
Manchester, N.H. 03105

Seton Leather Co.
849 Broadway
Newark, N.J. 07104

Superior Tanning Co.
1244 West Division Street
Chicago, Ill. 60622

Tilton Tanning Corp.
Tilton, N.H. 03276

United Tanners, Inc.
9 Orchard Street
Dover, N.H. 03820

Wisconsin Leather Co.
1830 South 3rd Street
Milwaukee, Wis. 53204

TOOLS—MANUFACTURERS AND/OR DISTRIBUTORS

Ace Hardware Stores
Local outlets

Always Tools
Bronx, N.Y. 10462

MacPherson Leather Co.
200 S. Los Angeles Street
Los Angeles, Calif. 90052
Leather and tools

C. S. Osborne
Harrison, N.J. 07029
*Catalog, price list, local distributors; all
leatherworking needs for shoemakers
and craftsmen*

Russo Leather & Finding Co.
1460 East 4th Street
Los Angeles, Calif. 90052
General supplies

United Shoe Machinery
104 Federal Street
Boston, Mass. 02109
*Manufacturers of complete line of tools
available at shoe findings and leather findings
companies; catalogs to the shoe trade*

Henry Westpfal & Co.
4 East 32nd Street
New York, N.Y. 10016
Catalog and retail store

X-acto Precision Tools, Inc.
48–41 Van Dam Street, Dept. 25
Long Island City
New York, N.Y. 11100

FINDINGS

American Specialty Hardware
Chattanooga, Tenn. 37400

Gordon Shoe Findings
2 McRaw Street
Roslindale, Mass. 02131

Jos. Hart & Sons
16 Reade Street
New York, N.Y. 10000

D. D. Holiday & Co.
15 St. George Street
St. Augustine, Fla. 32084

Martin M. Jordan Corp.
9 Murray Street
New York, N.Y. 10007

Kline Savidge Co., Inc.
163 3rd Street
Philadelphia, Pa. 19106

J.C. Larson Co., Inc.
7330 N. Clark Street
Chicago, Ill. 60600

North & Judd
New Britain, Conn. 06050

Ohio Traveling Bag Mfg. Co.
811 Prospect Avenue
Cleveland, Ohio 44115

Orville Leather Hardware Corp.
228 W. Chestnut Street
Orville, Ohio 44667

I. Sachs
637 W. Roosevelt Road
Chicago, Ill. 60600

Star Buckle Co.
3721 Chestnut
Philadelphia, Pa. 19104

Trinity Buckle Co.
P.O. Box 5169
Santa Monica, Calif. 90405

Waterbury Buckle Co.
Waterbury, Conn. 06702

CEMENTS AND GLUES

Barge Cement
100 Jacksonville Road
Towaco, N.J. 07082

Bordon Chemical Co.
New York, N.Y. 10000
Elmer's Glue

Du Pont de Nemours & Co.
Wilmington, Del. 19898
Duco Cement

Franklin Glue Co.
Columbus, Ohio 43207
Franklin Liquid Hide Glue

Master Chemical Co.
27 Bradston Street
Boston, Mass. 02100

Petronio Shoe Products
1447 McCarter Highway
Newark, N.J. 07100
Petronio Glue

Sanford's Elephant Glue
Bellwood, Ill. 60104

Tandy Leather Co.
Local listing
Craftsmen All-Purpose Cement

U.S. Plywood Co.
2305 Superior Street
Kalamazoo, Mich. 49003
Weldwood Contact Cement

DYES AND PIGMENTED COLORINGS

H. Behlen & Bros., Inc.
10 Christopher Street
New York, N.Y. 10014
*Behlens Aniline Stains;
Wood stains applicable to leather*

Fezandie & Sperrle, Inc.
103 Lafayette Street
New York, N.Y. 10013
Leather and batik dyes

Fiebing Chemical Co.
516 2nd Street
Milwaukee, Wis. 53202

Magi Dyes Co., Inc.
Linden, N.J. 07036

Master Chemical Co.
27 Brandston Street
Boston, Mass. 02100

Omega Leathercraft Products Co.
Fort Worth, Tex. 76100
and
Los Angeles, Calif. 90052

Permanent Pigments
2700 Highland Avenue
Cincinnati, Ohio 45212
Artists' acrylic paints

Rit Dyes
Best Food Co.
Indianapolis, Ind. 46206
Fabric dyes

R. Shiva
433 W. Goethe
Chicago, Ill. 60610
Artists' oil paints

Testor Corp.
Rockford, Ill. 61101
Craft paints

Index